VOLUME. 2
ON THE OTHER SIDE

by LINKED IN AND TOWN HALL ACHIEVER OF THE YEAR
EY NOMINEE ENTREPRENEUR OF THE YEAR
GRAND HOMAGE LYS DIVERSITY
WORLD TOP100 DOCTORS

Dr BAK NGUYEN, DMD

&

Dr. LINA DUSEVIČIŪTĖ DMD
Dr. DUC-MINH LAM-DO, DMD
Dr. JULIO REYNAFARJE, DMD

TO ALL THOSE LOOKING TO WALK THEIR DESTINY AND WANDERING WHY THEY ARE SO DIFFERENT.

by Dr BAK NGUYEN

Copyright © 2021 Dr BAK NGUYEN

All rights reserved.

ISBN: 978-1-989536-33-9

Published by: Dr. BAK PUBLISHING COMPANY
Dr.BAK 0059

DISCLAIMER

« The general information, opinions and advice contained in this medium and/or the books, audiobooks, podcasts and publications on Dr. Bak Nguyen's (legal name Dr. Ba Khoa Nguyen) website or social media (hereinafter the "Opinions") present general information on various topics. The Opinions are intended for informational purposes only.

No information contained in the Opinions is a substitute for an expert, consultation, advice, diagnosis or professional treatment. No information contained in the Opinions is a substitute for professional advice and should not be construed as consultation or advice.

Nothing in the Opinions should be construed as professional advice related to the practice of dentistry, medical advice or any other form of advice, including legal or financial advice, professional opinion, care or diagnosis, but strictly as general information. All information from the Opinions is for informational purposes only.

Any user who disagrees with the terms of this Disclaimer should immediately cease using or referring to the Opinions. Any action by the user in connection with the information contained in the Opinions is solely at the user's discretion.

The general information contained in the Opinions is provided "as is" and without warranty of any kind, either expressed or implied. Dr. Bak Nguyen (legal name Dr. Ba Khoa Nguyen) makes every effort to ensure that the information is complete and accurate. However, there is no guarantee that the general information contained in the Opinions is always available, truthful, complete, up-to-date or relevant.

The Opinions expressed by Dr. Bak Nguyen (legal name Dr. Ba Khoa Nguyen) are personal and expressed in his own name and do not reflect the opinions of his companies, partners and other affiliates.

Dr. Bak Nguyen (legal name Dr. Ba Khoa Nguyen) also disclaims any responsibility for the content of any hyperlinks included in the Opinions.

Always seek the advice of your expert advisors, physicians or other qualified professionals with any questions you may have regarding your condition. Never disregard professional advice or delay in seeking it because of something you have read, seen or heard in the Opinions. »

ABOUT THE AUTHORS

From Canada, **Dr. BAK NGUYEN**, Nominee Ernst and Young Entrepreneur of the year, Grand Homage Lys DIVERSITY, LinkedIn & TownHall Achiever of the year and TOP 100 Doctors 2021. Dr Bak is a cosmetic dentist, CEO and founder of Mdex & Co. His company is revolutionizing the dental field. Speaker and motivator, he wrote 72 books over 36 months accumulating many world records (to be officialized). His books are covering:

- **ENTREPRENEURSHIP**
- **LEADERSHIP**
- **QUEST OF IDENTITY**
- **DENTISTRY AND MEDICINE**
- **PARENTING**
- **CHILDREN'S BOOKS**
- **PHILOSOPHY**

In 2003, he founded Mdex, a dental company upon which in 2018, he launched the most ambitious private endeavour to reform the dental industry, Canada wide. Philosopher, he has close to his heart the quest of happiness of the people surrounding him, patients and colleagues alike. In 2020, he launched an International collaborative initiative named **THE ALPHAS** to share knowledge and for Entrepreneurs and Doctors to thrive through the Greatest Pandemic and Economic depression of our time.

In 2016, he co-found with Tranie Vo, Emotive World Incorporated, a tech research company to use technology to empower happiness and sharing. U.A.X. the ultimate audio experience is the landmark project on which the team is advancing, utilizing the technics of the movie industry and the advancement in ARTIFICIAL INTELLIGENCE to save the book industry and to upgrade the continuing education space.

These projects have allowed Dr Nguyen to attract interests from the international and diplomatic community and he is now the center of a global discussion in the wellbeing and the future of the health profession. It is in that matter that he shares his thoughts and encourages the health community to share their own stories.

"It's not worth it go through it alone! Together, we stand, alone, we fall."

Motivational speaker and serial entrepreneur, philosopher and author, from his own words, Dr Nguyen describes himself as a dentist by circumstances, an entrepreneur by nature and a communicator by passion.

He also holds recognitions from the Canadian Parliament and the Canadian Senate.

ABOUT THE GUEST AUTHORS

From USA, **Dr. Maria Kunstadter**, Doctor of Dental Surgery, co-founder THE TELEDENTIST, the biggest TELEDENTISTRY provider in USA. Experienced President with a demonstrated history of working in the hospital & health care industry. Skilled in Customer Service, Sales, Strategic Planning, Team Building, and Public Speaking. Strong business development professional with a Doctor of Dental Surgery focused in Advanced General Dentistry from UMKC School of Dentistry.

From USA: **Dr. Paul Ouellette**, DDS, MS, ABO, AFAAID, WORLD TOP 100 DENTISTS, Former Associate Professor Georgia School of Orthodontics and Jacksonville University. A visionary man looking for the future of our profession. Dr. Paul Ouellette Highly motivated to help my sons become successful in the "Ouellette Family of Dentists" Group Dental Specialty Practice.

From USA, **Dr. Jeremy Krell**, dentist MBA and serial entrepreneur, the real definition of an OVERACHIEVER. Highly experienced innovator and entrepreneur with a proven track record of taking early-stage startups to acquisition (multi-million dollar buyout). Excellent clinical dentistry and communication skills with in-depth analytical, organizational, and problem-solving abilities. A detail orientated and strategic leader in a dynamic, expeditious innovative environment. Firm experience with strategy, positioning companies, leading & developing teams, raising capital, investor relations, dental materials & techniques, negotiating & closing deals, and sales.

VOLUME. 2
ON THE OTHER SIDE

by Dr. BAK NGUYEN
with Dr. LINA DUSEVIČIŪTĖ,
Dr. DUC-MINH LAM-DO
& Dr. JULIO REYNAFARJE

INTRODUCTION
BY Dr. BAK NGUYEN

FORGIVENESS
CHAPTER 1 - Dr. BAK NGUYEN

FEARS
CHAPTER 2 - Dr. BAK NGUYEN

THANK YOU
CHAPTER 3 - Dr. BAK NGUYEN

THE 5 STAGES
CHAPTER 4 - Dr. BAK NGUYEN

THE DANCE OF DRAGONS
CHAPTER 5 - Dr. BAK NGUYEN

THE RISE
CHAPTER 6 - Dr. BAK NGUYEN

ABUNDANCE
CHAPTER 7 - Dr. BAK NGUYEN

HUMILITY
CHAPTER 8 - Dr. BAK NGUYEN

PART II
BY GUEST AUTHORS

THE ALPHAS TRAITS
CHAPTER 9 - Dr. LINA DUSEVIČIŪTĖ

I AM AN ALPHA
CHAPTER 10 - Dr. DUC-MINH LAM-DO

LIVING THE CHANGE
CHAPTER 11 - Dr. JULIO REYNAFARJE

CONCLUSION
BY Dr. BAK NGUYEN

INTRODUCTION
by Dr. BAK NGUYEN

This is a love affair! When I think of it, I wasn't sure of the subject at first, when coach Jonas proposed to write about Alphas. In less than a week, I finished my part of **AMONGST THE ALPHAS**, nearly 22,000 words within 8 chapters.

I started that book as strong as I could, talking about my experience as an Alpha, my journey of becoming an Alpha. Quickly, I followed my instincts, and the writing brought us into a new direction, one that we did not expect.

Coach Jonas had in mind a testimony and secrets to share. Instead, the **BOOKS OF ALPHAS** was more a philosophical one. I, myself, have evolved within the writing of the book on my views about being an Alpha.

I blew everyone's mind and went ballistic with the origins of the **ALPHA GENE** and the hope that everyone could be an **ALPHA**. We aren't born **ALPHA**, we choose and grow into one.

It took me 6 chapters before I finally shared with you my journey and discovery as an **ALPHA**. Then, by chapter 7, philosophy and the power of the possibilities empowered the best of me. This was just the beginning of something, not the conclusion!

I confirmed that feeling, writing the 8th and last chapter of the book. Usually, I will develop one subject, but there was still so much left unsaid, and many of Jonas' questions that I did not address. I packed within the last chapter all the remaining questions.

It wasn't the best course of action, to condense into one single chapter all of the remaining questions, but the subject was one of too much importance for me to simply skip those questions.

This was yesterday. Then, I woke up this morning with more to say on the matter! I wasn't sure if the right choice would be to add another chapter… but I wanted to keep mine at 8, the numbers of the dragon, the infinite numbers.

> "Alpha, dragon, infinite, that was my way
> to greet you with fortune and hope."
> Dr. Bak Nguyen

I always care for my readers. About a subject? Well, as soon as I said what I have to say on the matter, I have to tell you that I do not get too attached. Usually, I move on to the next book, the next subject. But the **ALPHAS**, it is the first time in my career that I was still thinking on a subject the day after I close the writing. Do I care that much about **ALPHAS**?

Truth be told, I do now. What was a label to me, after chapter 7 of tome one, the evolution of the Alpha and how important it is to humankind as a species, well, I couldn't cut it short.

Now that you know that being an **ALPHA** is a choice open to everyone, that you are motivated to start your journey, it wasn't a good time for me to simply jump to another subject.

So here comes **AMONGST THE ALPHAS, vol. 2 - ON THE OTHER SIDE**. This one will be a little darker than the first volume. We will be exploring **what if**, you do not step forward, now that you've seen the horizon. What would be if you try to bury your head back in the crowd and the average?

> "Once a mind touches a higher level of energy, it will never go back to its original level."
> Albert Einstein

I woke up this morning on the words and the imaging, it was too vivid to pass. This is what I woke up to. I drafted 4 chapters out of 8 already. About the other half? Well, I will let it be for now, so I will have space to grow into.

> "The more I write, the more I learn, and the more I have to share with you."
> Dr. Bak Nguyen

Of course, I will invite the Alphas to join me on this second tome too. To prove my commitment to the Alphas, I published this morning the cover of **AMONGST THE ALPHAS volume 2** on the social networks. And you all know me by now, I walk my talk!

To be honest with you, most Alphas learnt about the 2nd volume at the same time that the rest of the world was visiting my stories and post. It is a positive kind of pressure, a friendly one.

You wanted to know how **ALPHAS** act amongst each other, well this is a perfect example, while the average will expect communication, dealing, compromising before announcing anything, well, amongst **ALPHAS**, we challenge each other. Always with respect.

And what happens if one is not available for the challenge? He or she will simply declines politely, once again, with respect. Do you have any idea of the time saved, challenging each other, instead of asking for permission?

The worse that could happen is that some Alphas will be declining this invite and I will write alone. But I know the Alphas, they will never decline a good challenge.

Is this pressure, peer pressure? Well, sure, it is inspiration, intimidation and peer pressure all at once. It is also empowerment, leverage and caring, much caring!

We met each other under different circumstances. We are very different and from different cultures and parts of the world.

What unites us is the respect we have for each other and our commitment to take an active role in our world, in society.

In front of an Alpha, be careful what you wish for, since it might happen sooner than you expect. But before we can change the world for the better, we must first understand who we are and how to find synergy.

I will surely find much pleasure reading about the Alphas and what my colleagues will have brought from their perspective. As usual, I will be playing my part, opening the journey and leading the way into the unknown.

This is how I keep myself motivated and eager for more because I do not know what will be coming next, until I walk the first steps. And, as I do, my pleasure is to map and to figure things out as soon as possible, but leaving an opening for the unexpected. Well, with Alphas joining me, the unexpected is now part of the expectations.

Welcome to the Alphas. This is **AMONGST THE ALPHAS vol. 2 - On the other side.**

Dr. BAK NGUYEN

CHAPTER 1
"FORGIVENESS"
BY DR. BAK NGUYEN

By now, we know that the first step to embrace your **ALPHA GENE** is to start dropping your fears. Easier said than done! Let me be perfectly clear, keeping your fears close to you, won't do you any good. If anything, it might harm you more than you ever imagined.

The title of this volume is **ON THE OTHER SIDE**. But there is more than one side. For those who crossed the mirror and became **ALPHAS**, the story is the one that most of us read in volume one… and maybe in volume three.

But, for the majority of us, we won't be jumping by the first day we knew that there was something else, an alternative to our small lives. We will look in the mirror, see the possibilities, grasp the air for a minute or two, and turn our heads back to what was.

ON THE OTHER SIDE, is for those of us who had the information and are still reluctant to jump. You too have changed. Not becoming an **ALPHA** right away, but your awareness of the possibilities will make it impossible for you to go back asleep as you were before.

 The first thing that you'll notice is the weight of the fears you are bearing on you back, each day, day after day. I am sure that there are good reasons why you do not drop those fears, but now, you are very aware of the burden they impose in your life.

The longer you'll wait to take action, trying to ignore that awareness and faking life, as usual, the more harm you are doing to yourself. Not for bearing the burden, you've done that all your life, but because each day passing with awareness, is a day more that you condition your mind and character to accept to lay down your head and aspirations.

This by itself, will be a burden even heavier to bear. I saw people trying to adapt to that condition. Their back will break under the weight if not, it will curve slowly, but permanently toward the bellybutton to close the loop.

The neck too, will follow the trend. Eventually, the only thing they will have left is the possibility to raise their eyes to look up. And the light coming in, well, that once inspiring and liberating light, that same light is now a painful reminder of what could have been.

"There is nothing worse than regret to break a spirit."
Dr. Bak Nguyen

And once broken, the chances of coming back are shattered. The longer the wait, the smaller and numerous the shattering and the pieces. Eventually, one will never be whole again.

This is the human conditioning from **Conformity**, from Society. As we are born and trained, we've been curved and shaped into **bonsai** to fit the needs and requirements. The results are sometimes pretty, sometimes useful, other time, trivial. It all depended on the needs of Society by that time, that trend.

Since **Conformity** and Society don't know how to create, all they could do is to carve a sculpture out of us, a **DIAMOND IN THE ROUGH**, that's how they called us before they started the amputation and the friction process.

The reality is that you were a block of ice in which they carved out more than half to find what they deem beautiful and useful. The rest is still part of you, but is now laying on the ground, bloody and deem useless. That's half of your soul, half of your life force, that is rooting on the ground.

And that amputated half, well, they will clean it up and give it back to you in a pretty box, a masked cage for you to hide away. You have been initiated.

It was an honor and a privilege, but the pain couldn't lie. How the hell could you come to terms with that? You never did, only your mind and body chose to forget since the pain was unbearable.

Then, they welcomed you into their ranks, presenting you with rings and necklaces, all shiny and precious. You wear them with pride, showing them to the world, one in which you look like the others.

When you looked in the mirror, what did you see? You saw the necklace for what it really is, a chain tie to your neck. When you look at you rings, what do you see? Weight holding you down. This is wrong, the mirror is broken, you told yourself.

Then, you look back at Society and cannot unseen the chains on everyone's neck. They are walking tall and pride, but they all have that chain around their neck!

Look closer. Now, you recognize the scars of the faces and bodies of everyone, every single person. No one has healed, the sites of amputation are all screaming in silence, but no one seems to hear them.

And the more you look at them, the scarer you are to look back in the mirror. You will even start to avoid their eyes, fearing to see yourself in the reflection of their eyes.

What you see is a reality, not the truth. It is perfection through the eye of **Conformity**. You do not have to agree with it, you do not have to like it, you just have to bear it, proud or not!

What kind of bullshit is that?! In the past, we called then eunuch, those we castrated for the need of Society. Even today, that's how we "**control**" the behaviors of our pets, those pets we loved so much.

That's not love, that's torture and cruelty wrapped in Saint-Valentin paper! This isn't life, it is Society!

There are not 5 different ways to do this. You can either lower your head for the rest of your sentence, or you can cross the mirror. I won't lie to you, what you saw will be forever etched in your mind, but that's only one reality, there are other possibilities.

> "The universe is abundant.
> The truth is vast and contains many realities."
> Dr. Bak Nguyen

Just like you, I was forged and **bonsai** by **Conformity**. Just like you, I've been amputated and lost my wings. I was bigger, so they carved more out of me to fit the mold. They only let me out the day I could pass through the door.

They did so, keeping me alive. On the outside, I look like everyone else, but on the inside, they left a big bunch of raw stuff untouched. They left me my happiness.

That happiness helped me to move on. The amnesia from the pain was a success and had its intended effect. But from time to time, I heard voices, ghosts in my sleep, even when I was awake. And the voice, it was scary, but as I listened more carefully, I recognized my own.

Each time the pain came whispering, my happiness and my laugh masked the ambience. It was just like in the horror movies when the ghost and the darkness hit, I closed my eyes and went to my happy place, laughing.

Until the day I met with a mentor who taught me how to heal. He said: "You have to forgive yourself." At first, I did not understand his words… but years later, **FORGIVENESS** was the map to the masked cage that I hidden and forgot.

I went back and opened the box. Inside, everything was still there, bloody, smelly and hideous. Those were amputated wings and part of my soul. I was afraid and shouted the box. But it didn't close, the smell of rotted blood followed me everywhere I went after that.

After a few days sleepless, I reopened the box and let the fresh air in. I left the box open, and the smell slowly faded away. With air and light, the parts started to heal themselves. I picked up the limbs and cleaned them.

I held them close to me, they were parts of myself. They are me. I am not really sure of what happened next, but within days, the box emptied itself, and the smell was gone.

> "Forgiveness heals all wounds."
> Dr. Bak Nguyen

Only then, I understood the wisdom of my mentor. And then, my reality started to morph. I could fly! Barely at first, but my wings, they were attached to my back. I could fly, I just need to learn how.

I look in the mirror, and I wasn't the same anymore, I was whole! So I learnt to use my wings and to embrace their power and freedom. Every day, day after day, I spread them and trained by myself.

That's how I successfully achieved more within my last 2 years than my first 40! To the world and to you, I embraced the **YESMAN CHALLENGE**, to me, it was me exercising my wings and my soul, now whole.

Only then, I knew that I became an **ALPHA**. My **wannabe** phase are those moments where I heard the voice and saw the ghost. I react to them, but only for a brief moment. For a brief moment, I thought that I was whole, and then, faded away as the box closed itself down. The only thing I had left to hide the awkward feeling was my laugh and happiness.

With time, I mastered that art of **rebooting** the vibe and setting it to the tone of my laugh, and eventually, to the tone of my voice.

But then, the voice came back even if the box was shouted and hidden away. I followed that familiar voice, not knowing that it was mine. I became an **arrogant**.

Arrogant since I questioned why and why not. Arrogant since people don't have answers to my questions. Arrogant because my questions were glimpses of the mirror showing a reality that everyone refuses to see.

But they saw, for a brief moment, the vision and the reflection, the chains, the scars and the amputations. Each time, they blamed me for the bad vibe and my imagination. I was an arrogant and I was undesired. Once again, what I had left to cope with was my laugh.

Laughing and happiness kept me alive and healed me through every turn. And trust me, both the smile and the laugh were genuine. If not, I would have never made it through.

I survived happily **Conformity** and **Society** for 40 years, laughing, editing my story and most of all, forgetting the pain and the past. I survived, but I wasn't whole.

Only when I started forgiving myself for having accepted the amputation of half of my soul that I started to heal. I thought I was growing, well, looking back at the events, I was becoming whole, reunited with my wings and amputated soul.

The scars are there, somewhere, but I don't see them anymore. Maybe, I grew used to them. The cure and medicine that put me back together is forgiveness. Then, my spirit took care of the rest.

With my wings back, I flew, higher and higher. Each day passing, I flew a little further, a little better. That power became my **speed** and eventually grew into my **Momentum**.

My mirror, I crossed the day I opened the box and cleaned my limbs. I looked back at those I loved, and I saw the chains on their neck.

I ran to them and slammed my fist on the wall to break the chains. I stopped as I saw the fear and anger in their eyes. They were holding their necklace with all their life force, looking me in the eye with terror: why would I hurt them as such? But I tried to free them…

For the first time in years, I felt was real pain feels like. I almost forget that pain and the odour of amputation… I look closely, and the skin and flesh grew around the chain. That day, I cried, and my laugh could not help me cope.

I resigned myself not to hurt them, not to free them and let them be in their reality. I came back, visiting, with love, with pain. If everywhere, my laugh has the power to raise the mood and set the tone, this is one of the places where I am powerless.

I am there, ready to free them. But I saw the look in their eyes, and I felt their pain. What they did to me, they were, and still are, convinced that it was the best thing to do, since they are doing worse to themselves. I love them for loving me. Because of that love, I will also refrain myself from torturing them in return.

You will never see me complaining, neither in person, neither in any of my books. Here, I am only sharing my pain and my regrets of being powerless from love, to free those dear to me.

But I did learn much from the experience. I never accepted the treatment. If I couldn't free them, I will at least save the future, my son. I hid my son from the atrocity and protected him as much as I could from the **amputations** and from **Conformity**.

I am sure that even with my best intentions, he still got hurt. But his wings, those, I showed him how to use and to hide, so no one would clip them away. Before they do, they will have to walk over my dead body first.

That's the gift I gave my son. He will grow whole and confident. He has much to learn, but won't be held down simply because he is broken and looking to heal. He will be whole to grow!

> "Confidence is sexy."
> **Dr. Bak Nguyen**

This is my personal story and the journey of my evolution. You too, will have to walk yours, with your pain and healing. Trust me, I saw the skin and the flesh growing on the chains. I wish I could forget, but I still see the look in those eyes, looking back at me as the enemy, when I tried to free my loved ones.

The longer you wait, the harder it will be to free yourself and heal. Flying can be terrifying if you spent 70 years growing roots around the iron of the chain. It is a choice, one we must respect.

It may be okay if you are still living your amnesia, but that won't last forever. Sooner or later, you will have nightmares walking up in the land of the living dead, with zombies walking around and monstrous deformities angry and scary.

Well, look closely, the zombies, you know them by their names. The deformities, look at their heart, you will eventually recognize one as yourself.

You wanted to know what real love feels like? Go to that deformity you've recognized, and embrace it with all of your love. Ask for forgiveness and forgive yourself for having accepted to be treated as such.

Soon enough, you will wake up from this nightmare. As **FORGIVENESS** will heal all of your wounds, the sun will empower you to spread your wings and to look up. Drop your burdens and start flying, higher and higher.

And once in the air, if you look up, you go up. If you look down, well, you know which way that's heading!

Welcome to the Alphas. This is **AMONGST THE ALPHAS vol. 2 - On the other side.**

Dr. BAK NGUYEN

CHAPTER 2
"FEARS"
BY DR. BAK NGUYEN

And why should you drop your fears? Think of it for a minute, what are your fears, really, what are they made of? Most of your fears are the ones you've received as your legacy package, if not from your parents, from Society.

What they fear, you will too, if you hang around for long enough. But wait a minute, what they fear is what they could not conquer, control, or understand.

> "That was back then, haven't we evolved since?"
> Dr. Bak Nguyen

This has been a truth from the beginning of time, at least of Mankind. We are evolving, today faster than ever! So is it still relevant to fear what we feared yesterday? And those of a generation earlier?

It doesn't make any sense, but yet we are still transferring our fears down from one generation to the next. It would seem that we hate our children and future: we are amputating them, clipping them of 50% of their life force and potential, and then, just like it wasn't enough, we burden them down with the limitations of the last generation. Sometimes, we go even further back.

Actually, it is the other way around. We started by burdening them with legacy and then, as they are pinned down by the weight, we started clipping away their wings and excess limbs. We do, or we let Society do it, it is pretty much the same thing.

If that's what you called roots and legacy, well, thank you, but no thank you. Our civilization has evolved much and grown into an age where it is possible to accept differences and diversity. **Conformity** and religion have lost much of their grasp upon Society. Today, it is more accessible to choose and to think for ourselves.

Don't get me wrong, the choice was always there, but before, the repression and peer pressure were much more a burden to deal with than today.

That's why we owe it to the past generations to do better, to keep evolving, and to raise the bar and lift the limits for the next generations.

Right here, right now, today, we are the **Present** where the **Future** and the **Past** meet. That's the **ALPHA CALL,** to honor our legacy lifting the barriers of the past, walking whole into the land of discovery and hope.

You won't be able to do so with your luggage from yesterday, not to mention those from your legacy. Take that analogy, would you travel the world with the luggage of your grandparents? Their clothes, their souvenirs, their pains? What about those of your parents? And uncle and cousins and siblings?

It does not make any sense, right?

Even your own luggage, who will have to select the one fitting you at that instance and for the occasion. If you can pack as such for a vacation, why do you carry around your legacy luggage for the rest of your days?

So it is with **FEAR**, you will have your own to deal with, why carry around those of your legacy? The **ALPHA JOURNEY** isn't an easy one. Are you strong and motivated enough to run with piles of luggage on your back, thinking that you can outrun the best and come on top of the tallest of challenges? There is positive thinking, and there is stupidity. Open your eyes.

> "Fears transmitted are mostly
> the boundaries of the last generation."
> Dr. Bak Nguyen

As I said before, today more than ever, knowledge and technology have enhanced our speed of evolution to a new era. What was impossible yesterday is a possibility today and will be a standard tomorrow.

We have come a long way, from the age of the hunter, where **DNA** was the main way to pass down the **GENE OF SURVIVAL**. There was a time where those fearful and cautious had a better chance of passing down their genes. But even then, they carried the **ALPHA GENE**, only, it wasn't active.

Natural selection facing scarcity went with the boundaries in place. Those boundaries have changed much since the beginning of Mankind. Scarcity has been addressed. We might not have enough, but nowadays, we have much more than we ever did throughout time…!

The fading of scarcity allowed the fading of **FEAR** and **authority**. That's how today, we have a chance to look and think of better things. In the pyramid of Maslow, as the primary needs are met, we can then, move up the ladders to address higher needs.

As to eat and to shelter, to reproduce, and to feel safe are met, it is time for us to matter. Well, since natural selection went soft on us with the **ERA OF ABUNDANCE**, of less scarcity, our poll of genes had a better chance to renew itself: not one in which only the fearful are left alive to reproduce.

With the **ERA OF ABUNDANCE**, the **AGE OF ALPHAS** is coming next. It is coming because we, as a society, a civilization, are collectively thinking, each at his or her own pace, of way to matter instead of fighting for survival.

More and more, the wars aren't those we fight for lands, but for ideas. The greatest battles aren't the one we fight on the battlefield, but the ones in our heart and the worse ones are the ones we fight in our minds.

That's the **AGE OF ALPHAS**, an age where we are confronted with facing our fears or bowing down to them for another generation. Transmission and legacy?

How do you explain the arrival and rise of the **MILLENNIALS**? A whole generation looking for more, faster and better, refusing to accept the chains and jewels of Society?

> "Millennials are evolution and natural selection proclaiming their progression on the pyramid of Maslow!"
> Dr. Bak Nguyen

The transition won't be easy since it is a shock and a melting of culture and beliefs. But those are the next generation, our future.

As a parent, I salute and embrace the evolution and general upgrade. As an experienced citizen, I will advise caution and respect the transition from one **ERA** to the next.

> "The future is always brighter, if not, what is the point of talking about it?"
> Dr. Bak Nguyen

My generation is the transition one, the one stuck between the **MILLENNIALS** and the old ones. We have received the legacy and boundaries of the elders. With the boundaries and limitations, we also received the tools to navigate through.

As we are entering the **AGE** of maturity and the Apogee of our life, we also have the privilege to witness the **FREEDOM** and **REFUSAL** to accept the fears and boundaries of the last generation.

As a **TRANSITIONAL GENERATION**, we are hybrids. We can either serve as a buffer absorbing the shocks and clashes of evolution or we can be the ones empowering it, provoking the change and to ease the way for the next generation. It is for us, each one of us, to decide our role.

Mark my words, either you decide for yourself and make a stand or Society will choose for you. We are all part of it. How? Is still for you to decide.

This is why the **AGE OF ALPHAS** is coming. Not just for the general transition, but also the **MILLENNIALS** and those following after them. The paradigm shift of Society is well advanced and will neither stop nor reverse itself.

More and more, we will have to face the choice of choosing for ourselves or of keeping the default choice made by Conformity for us. The youth will be making their own choice, getting them closer to their **ALPHA GENE**, why not us? Why not everyone?

I refuse to believe that only the next generation can be better. Every one can, if only, one has the desire and aspiration for more, for better.

Looking for food and shelter was looking at our bellybutton. Looking to reproduce is looking at the other's bellybutton and looking to seduce. Looking to matter is looking at all the bellybuttons surrounding us and looking to help.

This strategy is working, but not at an optimal pace. Evolution is pacing up, life is pacing up, so should we, all of us! Stop looking at bellybuttons and look up, at the horizon, at the sky, at the Universe.

> "With evolution, fear is growing obsolete."
> Dr. Bak Nguyen

That's not a hope, it is a fact. If fear itself is growing obsolete, so is its transmission. Drop the fears, not just for your sake but for the legacy you'll be leaving. Drop your fears to catch up with the pace of evolution.

Drop your fears even faster to lead the evolution into the **AGE OF ALPHAS**.

Welcome to the Alphas. This is **AMONGST THE ALPHAS vol. 2 - On the other side.**

Dr. BAK NGUYEN

CHAPTER 3
"THANK YOU"
BY DR. BAK NGUYEN

As you can see, embracing the **ALPHA GENE** is usually not a straight line. It is not like in the movies where we have clean cuts, and we jump into the next action scene. But when you stop and think about it, that's an excellent idea!

The best recipe is to look ahead, to move forward, and to never look back! Nothing new, that's old wisdom, ever heard of looking will turn you into a statue of salt? But we can't resist the temptation of binding with the past. No one can, without an external force pressuring him or her to move on.

> "To move up the ladders, you must step on the past, a solid past, and keep looking at the next step. Your head is aiming at the horizon."
> **Dr. Bak Nguyen**

Is there any other way? To stop and stare? To go down the ladders? Trust me, people are going down the ladders, they are pushed down, thrown down, but no one is willingly going down the ladders of life, of evolution.

So we know the recipe, to go up, to keep moving. So why are we so afraid to step up? Because it's hard to say goodbye to those who accompanied us on the last journey.

There is nothing to be ashamed of. We all have people we love and do not want to leave behind. They too, have left people behind to be where there are.

On the other hand, to honor their love and hope, we too, must say goodbye and move on, move up on the ladder of life until we become one with one of the steps.

Unless we fall down and become one with one of the lower steps, this is the **pinnacle of life**. Some call it the circle of life. Circular, spiral, or straight line, the journey is a continuation of steps and ladders.

The steps are moving too, but at a much slower pace than the one stepping on it. If you are moving faster than the pace of the steps, you are moving up. If you stop and stare, you are losing your velocity and will have to double down on the effort of catching your run.

But if you slow down to the pace of the steps, something special happens: you have the illusion to move forward while you have the security of staying still and stiff.

The feeling is a warm and safe one since you now have the time to look around and to analyze all the corners of your environment.

Very soon, you will have the desire to never leave that place. It is not paradise, but you have found your nice, your place in the universe, or so you thought. You will become a settler and will start to grow roots.

Your wings, your speed, your vision won't help you there. You hide them away until they atrophy, both from your body and in your mind.

> "Were angels a different species created by God or the relics of an old memory of our own kind?"
> Dr. Bak Nguyen

And the mutilations and amputations? Well, it takes continuous work to settle on a step. The step is alive and moving. As we settle, most of our effort is to try to keep things still.

There is no way one could do that by him or herself. So we network to find ways to compensate for the loss of our wings and power.

Those refusing to join, we mutilate and kill, as a society. And then, necessity and **small intelligence** will show us the way, if you mutilate a soul, you decrease its energy… With less energy, no soul is thinking of leaving. Even if he might have the thought, he won't have the strength nor the means to do so.

I do not know what were the intentions of those who founded the basis of civilization. Were they already amputated and were conditioned to repeat the same to the next generation, certain that it was the right thing to do? Or were they simply mean and control freak minds looking to create a subspecies from the human race.

What I can tell you is that human history is full of human sacrifices and cultural and social amputations that we banalized as means to a greater end.

> "We are a savage and cruel species."
> Dr. Bak Nguyen

You don't agree? How many species have we eradicated to be the dominant species? Did we eat each of them? If it wasn't the primal need to feed, why did we do so? When you kill for sport and pride, it can't be good. It is surely not kind nor gentle.

And what about the pets we love so much? Yes, even today, what do you think operating them means? You are cutting theirs genitals away for better behavior control.

We are still control-freaks, and now, we are even hypocrites about it. We are not any better than those who installed the practice.

> "We love eunuchs as pets
> since it is our way to feel superior."
> Dr. Bak Nguyen

Are we that small of a mind? Can we be better? Don't you want better? Even our medicine is based on the same principle, to cut out. Sure, we heal with medicine and drugs, but ask all western doctors, what is the basis of his or her science? To identify and kill.

We are treating our body as a battleground with troops, reinforcements, and enemies. The enemies are the invaders that we must eradicate if we do not want to lose control, to lose the battle.

The recipe to modern medicine is to identify (diagnosis) and to treat (drugs). The reinforcement, if needed, is amputation (surgery) or eradication (chemotherapy and radiotherapy). Then, to replace what we cut off, we developed transplants and external enhancements. This is the basis of our science and the ultimate advancement of our doctrine.

I am not disputing the science here, I was trained as such, and I am not smart enough to present an alternative to this philosophy and doctrine. What I am pointing out is our cultural presence of cutting out to keep control.

> "Western medicine is mainly to cut and to replace."
> Dr. Bak Nguyen

Medicine is not the only field with deep stigmas. Look at agriculture and how we are treating the soil we settle on: with pesticide and war machines we've developed since the first and second world war.

Everything that is not a straight line, we kill, mutilate and eradicate. We do that to the Earth, we do that to the other species, we are doing that to our children and to ourselves.

> "I will just say that we can be better."
> Dr. Bak Nguyen

No, we won't be seeing all of this as we embraced the **ALPHA GENE** for the first time, but as we stop looking at our bellybutton, the horizon will show us more, and we will eventually see the truth as we look up.

The choice was made when you embraced or not, your gene, but now that you've touched it, it is too late to undo your awakening.

You will feel much pain, seeing your old reality for what it really is. Until you can make peace with it, you will keep bearing the suffering, the scars, and the pain.

You will have to come to terms with your new reality, to move forward and to rise up, cutting your flesh and the roots attached with the chains you cherished. This won't be your last amputation, but this one will free you to become whole again.

To self-amputated is one of the hardest things someone can put him or herself through. But, that's your legacy as a human and your birthmark as an **ALPHA**.

And is it worth it to move on forward with pain and anger, in our heart and body, to rise to the next level and keep bearing the mark of cruelty and violence that got us to evolve in the first place?

> "We are part of our legacy until we fill it with our choices and achievements."
> Dr. Bak Nguyen

The only thing I could say is that we can be better. We must try to be better, if not, all the pain will have been for nothing. This is just like when we went back to those we love, and try to free them while they are looking at us as murderers, wanting to amputate them.

From our point of view, we tried to free them. From their point of view, they do not see the chain over which their skin and flesh have grown.

Let them be. Kiss them and be gentle. The love you have should be one of respect, of respecting their wish. Don't even bother to tell them the truth, those words of yours will feel like razors in their throats and ears.

Be kind, embrace them, hide your sadness and show them the way by rising up yourself. If they come to you later, asking how, show them, with kindness, one step at a time.

This might sound selfish, trust me, it is not. It is kindness and wisdom. I tried the other way, and the results aren't pretty.

> "Naivety can be cruel
> and hurt even more than madness."
> Dr. Bak Nguyen

And what is naivety if not selfishness, to see the world only from your point of view? Remember, there is only one truth, but there are many, many realities. Until one has risen, reality and truth are one and the same.

But how do you cope with such pain and separation? How do we rise up with hope for better with such bitterness? The only answer I found is in **GRATITUDE**.

> "Gratitude is the only past with a future."
> Dr. Bak Nguyen

This is one of my favorite quotes since I started writing. The more I write it, the more sense it makes. **FORGIVENESS** allowed the reunification of my soul, and from being whole, I found my powers.

Not everyone is ready for such power. Not everyone can even stand the presence of such power, and the power of the Universe is vast and abundant.

In other words, the more I open up myself to the Universe, the more I grew stranger to those I love. If I cut all the ties, I will have started a new chapter, but with the same violence and ungratefulness than what I am running from.

I can't take them with me, since they refuse to leave their reality, even if they are miserable in it. To them, the insurance of being miserable is better than the risks of the unknown. It can always get worse according to them.

Well, I have to paint a new reality looking at them. Since there are no future possible where both visions can co-exist, I simply paint a reality and portrait of the best they gave me.

No hope, no expectation, but only the love and joy they gave me when I was their hope for a better future. This is called the **power of the narrative**. Make it into a compelling story, embellish it, forget the darker parts, and soon enough it will become a new reality. This is not lying, it is kindness at its best.

> "The truth can be cold and hard, not everyone can survive it, that's why we created realities."
> Dr. Bak Nguyen

Out of love and respect, I keep the smile and hide the sadness. I respect their choice and won't be pushing them. Not just to those who raised me, but also to the places I grew up in, Society itself.

I choose to make peace and to stop the amputations and violence. I choose to see past the torture and atrocity, the trauma and the pain. I am still a product of that society, and, if anything, I awoke in reaction to its presence and influence.

If anything, I choose to see Gratitude and to honor the good I received. I choose to erase and forget the pain. Even the scars are fading now that I started healing.

> "Healing doesn't mean to amputate
> and to learn to live with less."
> Dr. Bak Nguyen

THANK YOU is my magic word. Thank you for your love. Thank you for your training. Thank you for your expectations, yes, even your expectations.

Right and wrong do not matter anymore, saying thank you and choosing to keep the good was the only way to move forward **gracefully**, with **Gratitude**.

And soon enough, you will feel the **POWER OF GRATITUDE**, one that will bring back the colors, the tastes, and the joy to a prison made of blood, iron, and flesh. It does not have to be dark just because you were sad. Keep that in mind.

The magic of the multiple realities is that the mind can paint over everything and give it the illusion of our feelings.

> "Dark is sadness painted, cold is regrets painted, don't impose yours."
> Dr. Bak Nguyen

This isn't a lie, nor hypocrisy, it is a choice and a reality. That's the power of the mind, one that all of us possess. So, be gentle and kind, give them your love, painting their reality with your **Gratitude** and **joy**.

Smile and give them the satisfaction that they were right to love you. Be kind not to step on their chain, since it is their flesh and skin you'll be stepping on. It does not have to be a farewell.

You can always come back to that happy place, one you created and shared with them, now and forever.

> "The journey of the ALPHA is a lonely one."
> Dr. Bak Nguyen

You have to accept your choices as you learnt to respect theirs. I told you that the Universe is abundant, it is because there is a place for many diversities, many realities, many choices.

> "The smallness of a mind is to accept only what it understands."
> Dr. Bak Nguyen

Fine, if our minds can grow fast enough, at least, open them up so the air and the Universe will take care of its growth. But the heart? Open up your heart, and you will feel how big and vast, how abundant and kind you could grow.

And from your heart, the inspiration will be pumping through the rest of your cells and back. Keep your heart open, clean, and kind, and abundance and power will always be within you.

That how I chose to rise, with kindness and with respect. That started with a **THANK YOU** and with a smile. The awakening was only step one, and unlike in the movies, the cut isn't a clean one.

That doesn't mean that you have to perpetuate the challenge by hesitating or by reacting with your legacy, your old habits. Leave the violence and amputations behind, rise up and let go of what needs to go. Then, reunited with yourself, your soul, your whole.

What's good for you isn't good for everyone. You chose to rise, that's how you can bear the pressure and the heat. Ever heard the phrase that it will get worse before it will get better? Well, you chose so, respect your choice.

On them, on your past, paint the best portrait of **Gratitude** and souvenirs you can and smile. Embrace them for what they gave you, for what you see good in them, and let go of the rest. For all that you know, that can be their **happy place** for a while.

It is time to go. You know it, and they know it too. Leave the doors to the happy place open, you can always come back. That **happy place** is the only past you can look back at, without turning into a statue of salt.

That portrait is painted on **GRATITUDE**, and is named **THANK YOU**.

Welcome to the Alphas. This is **AMONGST THE ALPHAS vol. 2 - On the other side.**

Dr. BAK NGUYEN

CHAPTER 4
"THE 5 STAGES"
BY DR. BAK NGUYEN

That's the destiny of the awakener, the **ALPHA.** You can't look back although all you knew is behind. You can't unsee what you saw and now that you saw, you can only move forward. No one is forcing you, but yourself.

It's like you always knew, but a filter kept the voice like a distant echo. Only through your dream and pocket moments of lucidity (they call daydreaming) is that voice surfacing to your conscience.

Conformity and Society programmed you well after the **AMNESIA**. They gave you the illusion of freedom when, in truth, they gave you the choice of **what fear to lock in your heart**. They even gave it a pretty name and a glamorous face. They called it **LOYALTY**.

Blind **LOYALTY** to an idea is called **FAITH**. Actually, it is to a **GOD**, but since no one who has seen a God is left alive to tell the story, they will have you believe to take their words instead. I believe in God, I do not simply believe in the lies of those men looking for control.

LOYALTY to the land is called **PATRIOTISM**. Well, that's a great one, we gave names and delimitation to part of the Earth we are living on. They told us to be **LOYAL** to that part, but what about the Earth as a whole? What would you call that **LOYALTY**? Since there is no control possible, they left it out from the equation.

LOYALTY to your family is called **LOVE**. So if we love, why in God's name, are we looking to attach everything permanently in ties where the knot is the burden that kills love itself?

I'll tell, it is not about control, but about insecurity. Insecurity and ignorance. Those with insecurity and ignorance are those looking for control to survive. And the price for control, well, it isn't just **freedom**, but also **genuineness**.

Can love be forged?
Can friendship be bought?
Can desire be boxed?

To those, we all know the answer
So, they started carving us down,
Into manageable size and energy
So **LOYALTY** could be forced.

But those are, Society and Conformity, not nature. And nature is gentle and flexible until it reacts. You saw the storms and the tornadoes, but you also saw the wheat and the Sun.

What happens to a flow of water that you block? It will accumulate. While accumulating, it creates lakes and seas, until it floods and creates new rivers. Violence is not always a conclusion of nature, but it will react properly to any intervention.

Water also has a kind way of absorbing the initial shock as smoothly as possible. It is only when that flexibility and adaptability are breached, that water will react with violence instantly. We should learn from that.

The human spirit is one that can bend and stretch beyond our own comprehension since we are much more powerful than we've been told. On top of that, we do have the ability to network and to take it over where the last one left.

> "Networking gives us the means to bridge through space and time."
> Dr. Bak Nguyen

We should model ourselves on that part of nature, the **FLUIDITY**. That is actually the first lesson an **ALPHA** should master if he or she wants to be able to walk his path with results, lasting results.

But unfortunately, no one was there to show us the way. So most of us, if not all of us, will react with the only way we know how to react, will violence.

Facing the pain and the isolation, facing the fear of the unknown, and the impossibility to go back asleep, we will revolt! Each in our own way and intensity, but we will all revolt. That's the **WANNABE** stage.

Just like the 5 stages of grief, we will have to digest our awakening. First, we will deny the truth, thinking that it was nothing but a bad dream. But then, we will wake up in an even worse shape than we went to bed the day before.

Then, anger will kick in. That's the revolt and the expression of all of our long-repressed emotions. Keep a while animal, any animal in cage for a long period. What will happen when you open the door? As soon as there is an opening, it will blast through that slight opening and will run with all its strengths.

Keep looking, it will eventually slow down and stop. From afar, it will look back. It will look at you, right in the eye. From what it will perceive, it might keep running, never to come back, or it will return for you…

Now, what will happen if you open that cage in your living room? Well, it will just destroy everything in the process of stretching its newly found freedom. But just like water, if you leave it enough room to stretch, it will do so with much more fluidity, without breaking any boundaries.

Well, that beast you have released is your emotions. You've boxed them up and forgot about them in your basement for years. They lack air, light, and everything else, but they were still active.

Just like water running, they will fill up the box and build up the pressure. It is only a matter of time before the box will break down and release the accumulated pressure. And the longer you wait, the bigger the explosion, the flood, and the collaterals.

That's the anger phase. Especially when you went running back home to those you love and saw them for what they really are, prisoner and proud owner of their own prison. To not feel anger would be impossible.

So you will go out and cry at the top of your lungs the injustice, the pain, and the lies. Do that in your living room, and you will bring down your home with your loved ones' necks chained to the wall.

Do that in Society, at work, or at school, and you will break the **glass of Conformity** for a brief moment. They will all stop and look at you. Then, they will send reinforcement to bring you in. You are damaged goods, and they are people that will fix you…

The only thing you've accomplished is to break the **seal of Conformity** on your forehead and paint a target on your back. Don't be naive. People will just keep moving, you were an incident that tomorrow, they will have forgotten.

> "Anger and violence will only deepen
> your pain and suffering."
> **Dr. Bak Nguyen**

That's why I taught you the **POWER OF GRATITUDE**, to free you from your habit of bursting out and amputating. It is okay to let your emotions out. Actually, it is the only way to grow, but not in a controlled environment where every corner can be broken from the wind.

To your problem, there are two places that I recommend: nature and your mind. Nature because that's where you would take that cage before opening it up. What if your animal was a horse, a wild stallion, you would bring it in the valley and open the door, so it can stretch its legs.

If it was an eagle, you might climb the highest mountain before releasing it, so the first sight it will see is what it craved for so long, the horizon.

If it was a lion, well, the travel to the African Savana is the best way to have a chance for the lion not just to turn on you the minute you open the cage.

And the trip leading there, that time is much needed time for you to digest your fears and anger, to comprehend what you are going through, and to allow the reunification.

Don't get me wrong, that animal you caged, is a part of you, and it will be mad. It is already, you just won't see how mad until you open those doors!

But as you are climbing the mountain, driving through the valley, or reaching the Savana, you are making peace with yourself, that part you know. You are preparing to meet your other half, and when you'll do, at least one of them will be calm enough to absorb the rage of the other.

That's your first journey, the **WALK TO REUNIFICATION**. That one, you must do alone, since you are looking at connecting with parts of yourself you might know nothing about and which you have no idea how it might react. It is not safe to have other people around.

Your beast might hurt you, but you can take it. You'll have enough to deal with, not to care for collateral damages on top of your issues. Make that trip alone with your cage.

Nature was the first choice. Go to a vast place, an empty place where you can scream and think as loudly as you want and not break anything, not yet. Take the time to get there and prepare yourself for what's coming.

The other choice is your mind. If you have that reflection and the need of freeing your beast and opening up your cage, that's because you already free yourself from certain fears. You have awakened. In other words, your mind is opening up already.

You'll be surprised how far your mind can stretch and how much it can hold. I didn't take an exotic trip to open up the cage. I should have, but I didn't. Instead, I went deep into my mind and opened the cage.

Before I did so, I threw out as much as I could to be in a vast empty space so my beast could run and fly as much as it wants and not be able to break anything of importance. I went to sleep and opened the cage. That's how I slept with myself that night.

I woke up, and it was still there, running and stretching, not its legs and wings, but the boundaries and borders of my mind. I let it be. I even empowered it.

I let it be free for a while. And it came back to me. It took me a few years, but it finally ran out of anger, of fear. I ran out of anger, of fear. In the meantime, it did stretch my mind to an extend that even today, I haven't fully explored yet.

Then, I started writing. I made peace with myself, achieving and writing, doing and sharing, thinking, and scoring. We became one, reunited, me and my emotions, me and my beast. And since that day, I mount my beast and ride the day. My beast is a **tornado**.

> "Running out of fear and anger,
> I became one with my beast."
> Dr. Bak Nguyen

By that time, I ran out of fear, I stop being a **WANNABE**. Because I stopped trying to open the cage within my living room, my workplace, or at any public place, I stop caring about the collateral damages and the public relations.

I concentrated all of my energy on the reunification, the freedom, and the possibilities.

I think, and I score,
Me and my beast.
I talk, and walk,
Me and my beast.

I discover, and I am,
Me and my beast.
I do, and I share,
My beast and I.

That's what triggered the reunification. To think, was me, being whole allowed me to score it big. To talk and then walk with the force of my whole, not handicapped anymore at half my strength. To discover freely and whole, I am complete. I am happy.

I do my best, now whole, I have no more insecurity, so I share, also freely and openly. Well, sharing allowed me to grow exponentially. Only whole, I could be secure enough to share as much, and consequently, to grow as such. I became an **arrogant**.

Yup, the last part, the noble part, the sharing part brought me back to Society where things were still running as usual. Being secure and confident, people could sense a different presence, a genuine presence.

Since I shared, not my thoughts, but my achievements, my experiences, and the **HOW** and **WHY** I got there, I am no **WANNABE** that you can just put away anymore.

GENUINENESS and **HONESTY** are my trades, and those trades gained the respect and interest of the crowd.

I could have stopped there, and I would have found my peace. But the third stage of grief is bargaining. That's how I bargained, refusing to shut the door on my past and those I love. I shared my experience with you earlier.

> "Through hope and inspiration, I bargained my way out of anger and revolution."
> Dr. Bak Nguyen

I must say, I am pretty proud of my twist, facing an impossible choice, one that could have forced me to drop the knife and amputate once again a part of myself. I told you that I was looking for more, for better, I was not lying!

So from bargaining my way out of anger, I went from a **WANNABE** to an **ARROGANT**. Arrogant because what I say and share are usually above what people can touch, see and digest at their current level. But, they also felt the warmth, the authenticity, and the caring from my words and intentions.

That was my first book. And then, I liked the feeling of growing, so I kept writing, putting them at the center and only referring to myself as exhibit A, as an example. Since I write what I know, and for me, to know, I did first, that became my signature.

Well, 59 books later, I ceased being an **ARROGANT** somewhere on the way. I stopped being an **ARROGANT** and became an **ALPHA** the day I look beyond myself.

Writing helped me to skip the fourth stage of grief, depression. I am a positive person, and I take responsibility for my actions and failures.

Writing, I always took responsibility even if I had only 1% of the wrong, what good it would do me to talk about the other 99% if I could not act on them? So my recipe is to write, to make sense of it, and to rectify it.

For the last two years and a half, you shared the journey with me, from one chapter to the next, from one book to the next.

> "Making sense and taking action have the benefit of not leaving any free time for depression."
> Dr. Bak Nguyen

That's how I cheated the system and skipped the worse phase! Now, the fifth stage, **ACCEPTANCE**. Well, this is where the fun and the power kicks in.

I don't know by which book I switched from **ARROGANT** to **ALPHA**. I only noticed months later as you voiced up your support and show interest in my journey.

Until that point, I could see jealousy and hate from peers and old friends whispering that I was talking too boldly, too loudly, but before they could have a chance to voice their criticisms, they were reading about my achievements and exploits, on a new interview.

I did not have access to anyone else until you came along, you, my public, my fans, those I inspired and helped. You are here because there is something real, and, more importantly, something for you. This is what elevated me as an **ALPHA** because you are at the center of my interest.

Even my title, Dr. Bak, I kept the **DR** in front of my name to remind me of the nobility I learnt being a dentist for nearly 20 years: to put your interests before mine. That's what I brought back in philosophy, entrepreneurship, and self-development, to put you first.

All of that became more than words and books, the day my son, William Bak, 7 at the time, asked me to write a book with him. At 8, we started, and before he reached 9, we already signed 22 books together. We successfully did so because I put him at the center, not myself.

He picked up on the recipe soon enough. If you are watching any of his videos (yes, William became a video blogger on social media on his journey becoming an author with his dad), you will notice his wording and intentions, always about you, his audience.

What we did, none of us could have predicted nor even expected. We embraced the day, allowed ourselves to discover the possibilities freely, and we walked the path as father and son, having much fun on the way.

I may have skipped 1 stage out of 5. The day I accepted who I really was and my purpose in life, I found happiness holding my son's hand through my **ALPHA JOURNEY**. I didn't expect the company, but he offered himself, he was begging to join in.

I accepted gracefully, both my reunification and his company, and we broke the sound barrier together. Before he joined, I was just finishing a new world record of **writing 15 books within 15 months**. I was exhausted and proud.

Well, a month later, we scored 2 new world records together, writing 8 children's books within two languages (French and English) with illustrations together. WITHIN A MONTH!!!

And then, he wanted to keep the connection going... Three months later, I was announcing a new milestone, **36 books written within 18 months + 1 week**.

That happens because I accepted who I was, and my purpose in life. I removed my bellybutton from my field of vision, and I connected with the universe... and with William.

Now, there is another great effect to my acceptance. Since I put my **speed** and **Momentum** to empower William's desire of writing books and sharing with you, I also boosted William's evolution into orbit.

I started with him when he was 7. Actually, he initiated his journey when he asked to join in at 7. Since his birth, I've been very careful not to break his spirit and to keep feeding his confidence.

Well, looking at him, he never went through the 5 stages of grief before becoming an **ALPHA**, he skipped the first 4 stages to join in with **ACCEPTANCE**.

I do not know the stages that he'll be facing on his journey, but since he was never broken, he didn't need to be healed, since his wings were never clipped, he only had to spread them and learn to fly.

ACCEPTANCE is not even the right phase for him. To him, it was just discovery and fun!

> "I will show you. I won't force you.
> But I won't wait for you."
> William Bak and Dr. Bak Nguyen

That's our signature as father and son. A promise, a kindness, and an acceptation, all into a single signature.

And **LOYALTY**? Well, I love that word and what it stands for. But the only thing one can be loyal to, is to a cause, not to a person, since that person will be changing, and so are we. I will be loyal to my journey and my purpose, discovering and sharing back what I learnt.

No matter your issues and where you are within your awaking, know that there is light on the other side. Know that it will get harder before it gets easier. It is also a journey alone, one you can't bring anyone along.

Well, if my journey can bring you anything of worth, this is it: the hope that nothing is written in stone and that the odds will eventually shift in your favor as you keep pushing and walking looking up and ahead.

I gave you a map, I followed that map. The Universe smiled at me and decided that it will prove me wrong, and I went along with it! I accept it and leverage it!

To be an Alpha is also to have the humility to accept help and gifts on the way. I am grateful, I am happy and full of energy to keep discovering my journey, having fun, and now, with company on the way!

Welcome to the Alphas. This is **AMONGST THE ALPHAS vol. 2 - On the other side.**

Dr. BAK NGUYEN

CHAPTER 5
"THE DANCE OF DRAGONS"
BY DR. BAK NGUYEN

Although your transition from awakener to wannabe, from wannabe to arrogant and from arrogant to Alpha won't be a smooth journey, it is not all bad. Is it?

If you don't look back, you won't turn into a statue of salt and eventually, meltdown. It is written in the Bible. Well, that's not religion speaking, it is wisdom, wisdom reordered from the History of Mankind.

The most painful part is not to get uprooted and cut the chains, but to see our loved ones making love to and polishing their chains. The look in their eyes when you came back and tried to free them, that's the most painful. You do not heal from that pain.

And then, you are alone, isolate facing the unknown. Many times, the temptation will be great to simply bow down and to return to your place, your room, your box. But just like a newborn who left the belly of his mom, you can't go back in.

Now, it is just a matter of how long will you wanderer between the phase until you reach the top of the mountain. Being a wannabe is pretty much like walking through a thick and dark forest, with no map and no compass.

That forest isn't anything new, that's the forest we grew up in. But since our childhood, we grew roots, and never moved around. Our only way to explore and to taste the world was to grow our roots in the under ground and to grow our branches to reach the sky, or so they say.

Well, the minutes you start to awake, most of your roots, you have sabred, that what started your journey. It will be painful and liberating at the same time. Only by cutting down those roots, will you find the force to open the cage and to start your reunification.

To me, that key was forgiveness. To forgive myself, I cut down my ties, **GUILT**. What was surprising, is that cutting down **GUILT**, I also cut loose another part that was holding me down much of my life: **ANGER**.

Looking back now, it is strange how we choose to grow our roots. **Guilt**, **Anger**, **Fear**, **Loyalty** were all purged as I started to rise. Not completely and not without doubt and second guesses, but eventually, what wasn't cut down from the awakening, I shook it off later as I was walking. I must say that roots are different from one person to the next, but in the end, they are all roots tying us down.

> "To save yourself from pain, don't get attached."
> Dr. Bak Nguyen

To be, instead of to have, have you ever heard that one? Well, that's pretty good advice to follow.

Then, as you rise up and start your walk, they will all look down on you wondering why aren't you standing at your place? Then, you never learnt to move around, so of course, you will be clumsy and fall. Sometimes the only one who will get hurt is yourself. Sometimes, you will hurt someone else on your way down, even if that the exception to the rule.

But most of the time, you will be bothering all of them, since you are doing something they cannot, for whatever reason. The majority will simply judge you with a disapproving look. Some will go out of their way to spit on your face and to lecture you to go back to your place.

To that pressure, you will have 2 choices, either to bow down and look back at your bellybutton. By doing so, you will grow back your roots at a new place, for a little while.

You will self impose tortures and amputations to recreate that amnesia in which you were comfortable once. You have moved, have seen, but you haven't learnt anything useful… yet. You are a wannabe.

The other option was to look up and aim at the horizon. Doing so, eventually, you cease hearing the noise and the barking. Your feet still touch the ground, your belly is still at the centrefold of your vision, but you are living at a new frequency.

Vibrating at that new level of energy, you are suddenly free of your movements, of your thoughts, of your destination. You look back at yourself in the reflection, and the tree is nowhere near to be found. Your skin has thinned down, your roots sorted out, keeping the only ones you call legs.

And unlike what common wisdom will suggest, the more legs a chair has, the more it sill be solid; well, to keep moving and to speed up, it is not the number of legs and roots that will help, but how they coordinate together.

And all those branches pointing up to the skies, I first thought that just like my roots, I will have to sort them out and to cut those not useful.

By chance, I did not! I remembered how much I have the bonsai training back home, cutting each branch to the iron will of a single vision. I promise myself never to live that experience myself. My roots, I let them sort out which are strong and which are burdens.

You'll be amazed how the dead weight is sorting itself out by itself as you are walking, even more as you are speeding up. So I did not cut anything down, I just stop trying to hold everything together, I was focused on moving forward, always forward, and moving.

When it came to the branches, those were blocking my vision of the sun and the horizon. Should I cut them down, at least trim some of them to have a better view, an unobstructed one? I was about to do so when I stare at the horizon first, the branches weren't the problem, my belly was.

Those branches are my minds and my thoughts, why should I cut anything down. I pulled them aside and sort them out, just enough to free my vision. As I walk my journey and pace up the walk, I met a new friend, the wind.

To a tree, a wind is nothing new, but until then, I was always submitted to the wind and its will. When strong-armed by the winds, I reacted deeper roots, more roots. But now, I was the one creating the wind, by moving forward.

As a wannabe and an apprentice, I've learnt to play with that new power, just like a kid will learn to play with fire. I must say that the first winds I created were barely a breeze, nothing more. And then, as I pushed my walk, I met with the other winds, the ones you endure.

Going against them was not just hard, it was painful… and most of the time, unnecessary. My goal was to move forward, but without a compass, where is forward? My goal wasn't to move but to learn to move. So I stopped fighting the winds and let down of my pride.

Do you have any idea how fast you can move with the wind in your back? But then again, I was still submitting myself to its will. I got most of my limbs back, those cut down from Conformity. I also grew very fan of the feeling of the wind against my face, the one I created.

So I lifted up all of my being to race the wind in my back. It is not even a fair race. But I kept doing it, every chance I got until I became one with the winds, both of them, the one I was racing and the one I created running.

I ran faster and faster. It became easier and easier, and I kept pacing it up. And then, I stopped. For a moment, I could see both winds chasing one another. By stopping, I stepped aside and looked around. Like **two dragons** chasing one another, the winds kept spinning and gaining in velocity.

I was at the center of it, in the **eye of the tornado**. I can't describe to you the feel, but it is one of peace and calm, Serenity will be the word I choose to best paint the moment.

I look around, beyond the winds, and notice that even if I stopped, I was moving faster than ever, I just grew stronger and adapted to my new dynamic environment, speed.

> "The first real power I ever discovered
> is the SERENITY OF VELOCITY."
> Dr. Bak Nguyen

The **SERENITY OF VELOCITY**, in other words, the **peace of speed**. So far was I from the roots and the perfection, from the **bonsai** and the noise.

If you must know,
I was happy, genuinely happy
For as long as I could remember.
I felt myself for the first time ever.

That how I freed myself from the views of others and grew from a wannabe to become an arrogant. Now, I run so fast that no one even dares to look me in the eye talking without any support of the walking. They still hate me though, now more than ever.

Remember, when I told you to not open the cage to your repressed emotions in a small place? Well, I learned that from my own mistakes. The arrogance kept coming back because I kept going back to my old neighborhood. Those looking at me with the label of arrogance were those I know on a first-name basis.

So I stopped coming back, and I let the wind to lead the way. All those branches I didn't cut down, well they are my opening to the world. Where ever I go, I have them to help me discover and taste the new, the undiscovered, the horizon.

In plain words, those are my thoughts. The more I keep my mind open, the more I am able to understand the world, not the only reality with my feet firmly pressed on the ground, but the many dimensions of the Universe.

Since I freed my emotions
And dropped my fears,
I learnt to outrun the winds
And to merge with them as a tornado,

I discovered the **SERENITY**
And the **VELOCITY**,
I let go of my pride
And the need for control.

Since that day,
I can move from one reality
To the next.
I can walk from one world
Into another.

That day, I dropped
My insecurity.

I told you that we all grew up in a forest, thick and dark without either a map or a compass. Those we thought we had are nothing more than the description of the world looking at your feet with our bellybutton on half of the map. Well, there was a time that we believe that the Earth was the center of the Universe. Have we really evolved since?

So since much of what I learnt to oriented myself were misguiding or plain wrong, what good could I have to hold the security or insecurity that they provide?

I grew the confidence that serves me as a compass to walk the miles and see the horizons. Trust me, there is no better teacher, there is no better feeling.

To have resisted to bonsai my branches and my thoughts, I learnt to prioritize instead of choosing. To me, there is no more right and wrong, only left or right, until the next turn. I still have my sense of morality, but not one of fear of retaliation.

I understand that I am asking much of you, to follow this quest of yours, but trust me, it gets better. To undo all of the bonsai training, I embraced the **YESMAN's CHALLENGE** for 18 months.

Instead of cutting down, I opened up and added on. Some were different, some were just bitter and bad, and some were unexpected jewels. I grew from all of the experience. I grew stronger, bigger, wiser.

Each experience allowed my senses to express old and new feelings. Each encounter nourished my soul and rebooted my mind to keep absorbing and to keep opening up, more and more.

Well, if I gain power from the **SERENITY** and the **VELOCITY**, to keep myself opening up, I grew my confidence. In the **EYE** of the tornado, I came to terms with myself, with my discarded limbs now reunified, with my mixed emotions, with my own boundaries and limitation.

> "Velocity allowed me the time to heal."
> Dr. Bak Nguyen

And **Serenity**, well, it allowed me to see clearly the dragons chasing one another, as in an endless dance. It is peaceful and playful, fun and relaxing. Why would I ever want to stop that dance?

The faster they are running, the bigger my confidence grew. I now know who I am. I grew confident enough to let myself be free, to let go of insecurities.

> "When you dance with the winds, you are a fool to try to control them, just follow the flow and enjoy the dance."
> Dr. Bak Nguyen

That's how I let go of my need for **PERFECTION** and for **CONTROL**. Without those two, you will quickly find out that insecurity is a *made-up word*. And to free yourself from that made up burden will lift you up to new heights, even without your winds.

> "Perfection is a lie, and control, an illusion."
> Dr. Bak Nguyen

I was free, and I was happy. But I was still an arrogant.

Welcome to the Alphas. This is **AMONGST THE ALPHAS vol. 2 - On the other side.**

Dr. BAK NGUYEN

CHAPTER 6
"THE RISE"
BY DR. BAK NGUYEN

Well, this is so new to me, to spend chapter after chapter to describe the steps, the details, and the feeling of this great journey. Within my first books, I would have spent one paragraph, two at the most, to describe the idea, and to never look back.

By now, this is the second book of the series, **AMONGST THE ALPHAS**, but the subject has its roots since my first book, two years and a half ago. Since then, I believe then more than half of my books are somehow related to this subject, the **ALPHA JOURNEY**.

I first referred to it as the **ENTREPRENEURS** and their journey. Then, as the **LEADERS** and the **LION'S HEARTS**. That what I had so much fun writing with William, how can a chicken heart grow into a lion heart? By opening its mind.

And how can a **Lion heart** grow into a **Dragon heart**? By opening its heart. And then, how can a Dragon keep growing? By unlearning to learn new ways.

In parallel with writing those stories with William, I was running my course to heal and to ride my **Momentum** to new heights. He was growing, I was healing, and then I grew even more.

I had to pass through the 5 stages of grief and to go through my awakening, as hard as it was. I had to learn to forgive myself and to reunify. William, all he had to do, was to embrace the vibe and to spread his wings.

To preserve his confidence since his birth, that's what I blessed him with. To have him select his own fears, that's the luxury I gave him, freedom as a legacy.

To tell you the truth, I believe that the relationship wasn't unilateral. I received as much as I gave. My awakening was painful, but my contact with William dimmed down all that noise into tenderness and love.

I look at him, and I feel hope. I just had the decency not to formulate these hopes into expectations. I looked at him and saw the kind of man I feel that he will grow into.

And then, I saw myself reflecting from his eye to understand the kind of father I must be to inspire such growth, from a child into a good man. I put the pressure on myself. I was the means, he was my reason. That's how it all started, nearly a decade ago.

The three volumes of **THE BOOK OF LEGENDS** will tell you the story in detail. I was born ambitious and never took no for an answer. Becoming a father did not change any of that, but it showed me how far my talks were from my results.

Holding baby William in my arm at sunrise to feed him, gave me the chance to look at the sun to find inspiration, to find a reflection. That's how I saw how little I was. Was that being little or being small, that was for me to choose.

I chose, and the following years will show my resolution. That day, looking at my reflection in the sun, I chose to be little, but little can grow.

My mind was little, I opened it up. My heart was gated, therefore it was little too. I got rid of the gates and the gatekeepers too. My vision was limited, I embraced Life with confidence and hope each day. I discovered abundance and most of the universe.

My Desire was to see William better, bigger, and wiser than his dad. Well, William grew, and so was my **Desire**. My Will was to have hope and to spare him the expectations. I bear those expectations, to grow into the kind of man that will inspire his son to be more.

Well, growing both my **Desire** and my **Will**, I released much **Energy**. To that Energy, I reacted and danced with it. That's the dance of the dragons forming my tornado. But still, I could feel the resistance everywhere I went.

> "Do not revolt. The goal is to evolve without resistance."
> Dr. Bak Nguyen

The keywords here are **WITHOUT RESISTANCE**. If I went so far, walked countless miles, and suffered so many challenges that I can't even remember anymore, it has to be for something better than what I am leaving behind.

Well, those roots slowing me down, those thick skin and shiny armours that I received as a legacy, I came to terms with them, gracefully and with gratitude. I made the most of what I could and then, left them behind for someone else to find.

My fears, I leveraged them into **stepping stone**. Stepping stone, not cornerstones. Now, they are somewhere behind. My tools, I made the most of them, and as the journey changed, I cleaned and polished them, and left them behind for someone to discover.

I do so because I too, once discovered those on my way, from someone else before me. This is the main reason why I am writing and sharing with you, so you know where to find those tools, swords and shields, armours and leverage.

Throughout this journey, I used many metaphors to convey your senses and imagination, so you understand the feeling and the experience. But if I have to clarify the path, here is my gift to you.

A formula to comprise most of the notions we spoke about. A recipe to help you through your journey, wherever you are in that journey. A map that will help you save your day to see the light to remember your hope and dreams. I call it the **ENERGY FORMULA**:

$$\text{ENERGY} \propto \frac{\text{DESIRE}^{\text{WILL}}}{\text{VALUES}}$$

In plain words, it stipulates that the **ENERGY** available is proportional to your **DESIRE** exponential your **WILL,** divided by your **VALUES** (Identity).

Try it out, and you will find that the formula is universal and can be applied in all the situation. I dedicated a whole book on the matter, my 53rd book, **THE ENERGY FORMULA**. Look it up.

Now that you have embraced your **ALPHA GENE**, that you've started your journey, waking up, this formula will be of great use to you to empower and to ease your way.

Everything is Energy, we are Energy. Are we consuming Energy or are we producing Energy, that's for us to decide and to grow or not into.

We all started little, consuming Energy. If that's all we do, we will remain small and keep eating Energy. If we choose to open our minds, we will grow and consume even more energy. Energy will fuel our growth. If we keep growing our hearts, then we will start to produce Energy too.

Just like when I tried to outrace the winds in my back, I opened my hearts and started producing my own Energy. Instead of choosing, I kept both my mind and heart open to embrace it all. That's how I started the dance of the two dragons, forming my tornado.

That's a recipe for power, not one for enlightenment. There was more. I did not break the sound barrier only with a recipe of **speed** and **Momentum**.

My Energy grew as I started freeing myself from my fears at first, but also from my past medals. I became lighter and lighter to move faster and further. If the journey started with the Desire of being a better man, it only picked up the day I started dropping my fears and identity.

On the way, I kept that purge, with respect, gracefully and with gratitude, leveraging on my fears and liabilities, respecting the choice of others and those I love, painting them **HAPPY PLACES**, and move on with kindness and without breaking the glass nor bringing any walls down.

All of that would explain the rise and the growth, but not the birth of my **Momentum**. Today, I am a force of nature, and those are the words of the wise men I met on the way. What could explain such a rise?

Going back to the **ENERGY FORMULA**, I noticed that it was a trap within itself. The more you live and experience, the more your Identity grows, which will divide your Energy. The less you do, the more your fears and false beliefs will grow, burdening your Identity and values, so once again, less Energy.

The only way out was to move fast enough to beat your brain into sorting and classifying those into new values. But how can a man outrun a storm, each day, day after day?

Well, it was to network with someone else. To network, not to depend on. I found a way to beat the **ENERGY FORMULA**, putting someone else at the center of my **DESIRE**, my son William.

Since I wasn't the center anymore, I had my belly button out of the way and could see so much more, with such clarity! I leveraged all of myself, flaws, and the ability to move forward, dumping everything that wasn't of use.

To leverage gave me the obligation and opportunity to sort out who I was, my fears, and my abilities. **To leverage is an action, not a status**, so everything I was, became the **WILL** of the equation, with William as the **DESIRE**. And since I was dumping my fears and dead weights, I have lesser and lesser values to divide my Energy with.

> "The day I stop seeing my bellybutton, that day, I became an Alpha."
> Dr. Bak Nguyen

And that's what happened. All my 59 books are telling that story, a week at a time. Like any of you, I was born with, and from the **ALPHA GENE**. Like most of you, I've been forged and sculpt by **Conformity** to fill a need and a role in Society.

Do I really have to say it? Now that my bellybutton is out of the picture, so is most of the resistance, internal and external. I am not naive, where there is change, there will be fear, and with fear, there will be resistance… unless the change happens faster than the mind could process it!

Master the **Energy Formula** to grow your speed, and with speed, you have the power to clear the shadows and the fog, leaving you with the real challenge ahead. And each challenge is your chance to outgrow yourself.

Like every one of you, I was looking for my happiness and a sense in my life. For more than 30 years, I remained dormant, docile. I always knew that they were something else, a familiar voice telling me to look for more.

For more than 30 years, I ignored that voice. And then, the **ALPHA GENE** reappeared in flesh in front of me. Not just as a cold and distant reflection in the mirror, but as a baby holding my finger from all of his palm.

That touch reminded me of who I was and the choice available to me. His **ALPHA GENE** triggered the awakening of mine.

We all have different stories and different reasons, but the **ALPHA GENE** is the same. Same gene, same strength, same nature. We all have our preferences, but as life is created, we will experience the same connection, the connection to life at our origins.

This is something pure and visceral, something that **Conformity** has not found a way to corrupt and distort.

It was my way out. Find yours and go to your happiness. We were all **ALPHAS** once, we were all happy once, they are no reason why we should stay stuck we where are, at this moment.

Seriously, we were all born happy, and something broke on the way to force us to look for happiness for the rest of our lives. That's a reality, it does not have to be your reality. It is up to you to choose what your tomorrow will be about.

Seek your Energy, look for your happiness, and choose freely. That's the legacy you've received with Life.

Welcome to the Alphas. This is **AMONGST THE ALPHAS vol. 2 - On the other side.**

Dr. BAK NGUYEN

CHAPTER 7
"ABUNDANCE"
BY DR. BAK NGUYEN

What a great feeling! As we started this journey, not so long ago, volume one was a great introduction and motivation to go forward. Volume two is kind of the dark volume, having to go through the darkness, pain and regrets.

Well, I am glad to tell you that you are now through with the darkness and the sorrow. From now on, things will be different. Different, not easier, although it might feel easier thanks to your experience and speed.

Now that you've been through the awakening, and started your walk on the **ALPHA JOURNEY**, do you have any idea of what you can do? Do you have any idea of the kind of power you hold in your hands?

We are all unique and different, but let me describe my journey and what I discovered on the way, my powers.

As you all know by now, I was raised by my parents, who are first-generation immigrants to Canada. They were part of the elite of their country, but that's now passed. We had much to lose not to succeed.

So, just like their peers, they bet on the education of the next generation to gain back what they left behind. I was raised with the elites' standards and expectations while they were working day and night to meet month's end.

Do I have to tell you that failure was not a possibility on the table? They taught me to concentrate and to focus my energy on one task at a time. They told me to mind my own business, and to work as hard as I could if I want a better future.

Conformity, **religion**, and **Society** took care of the rest of the equation. The reason why Asian kids are usually liked by our education system is that they are conditioned to obey and to thrive on the given task. And do I have to add that we are perfectionist people?

So I learnt to focus and to concentrate all of my energy on a given task. Just like the sun can be turned into a beam to start a fire, that's what my parent and Society forged out of me. I became a dental surgeon, efficient and precise to the fraction of millimetres, literally.

I minded my own business and trained myself to reach their perfection. But then, I realized that perfection was a big fat lie! Every time I was getting close to it, they changed the rules and added more. The closest I could get was to establish a new standard, never perfection.

Even if I achieved things out of the average, the satisfaction, if any, lasted for a day at most. I didn't grow up in a family that believed in empowerment. They believe in pressure.

I kept my connection and love with them, I bowed down and tried their way… for more than 30 years. Then, I became a dad and held the **ALPHA GENE** in my arms for months, feeding him at sunrise.

Those early mornings forced me to look at my reflection, and to ask the hard questions, the real questions. From those quests, I met with a mentor who taught me **forgiveness**. That opened the way to my **Reunification**.

You see, I am a sensitive soul and a creative person. My parents and Society forged out of me a doctor, surgeon, and scientist. I managed to survive the training and came out on top. I was a powerhouse of rationality.

After the **Reunification**, I was both, rational and creative, both above standard. But something else happened too, serving my training from **Conformity** and **Society**, I also became a master adapting and leveraging with what I had in hand.

So within a few weeks, I regained most of my creative abilities while keeping my rational and deduction capabilities. Well, ever heard of **SYNERGY**?

Very quickly, I became much more than the sum of my creativity and rationality put together, I became something else, a perfect hybrid and more.

That's when I decided to leave my profession (dentistry) behind, and to reach for my destiny. I would have done so if it wasn't for my newly obtained powers, which I was still unaware of.

Forgiving myself allowed not only the Reunification of my soul but also to unscrew my neck. You see, I've been trained to have a laser focus vision, efficient and precise. But for it to work, I need a narrow point of view, a small mind.

With the Reunification, I was thirsty for more, for different, for bigger and better. By unscrewing my neck, I started to scan everything with my laser focus vision. Scanning the world, I learnt more than I ever imagined possible, even if I spent most of my life on the school's benches. That's how far my rational stretched to.

I am many things, but a small mind isn't one of them. So I rebooted myself saying **YES** to virtually everything for 18 months (officially, 12 months). That opened my mind and allowed me to open my horizon and field of vision at will!

> "Creativity works in many ways.
> One of my favorite is to react
> to the world as I see it."
> Dr. Bak Nguyen

By opening up my mind, I could see more, I could learn much. By opening up my heart, I successfully kept my mind open for good. Usually, that would mean losing my laser focus faculty.

This is where the magic of the **ALPHA** happened: as my mind stayed open, I gained much flexibility and elasticity on my depth of field. Being an Alpha, I can now easily shift from wide to narrow within a second. I scan the realities, make sense of them and then, laser focus on the solution that needed to be implemented.

My creativity serves for more than just drafting the future and new possibilities, it also allowed me to get out of the box and to solve real and present matters.

I gave you all the formula and recipe within the first two volumes of **AMONGST THE ALPHAS** to follow in my footsteps and to find your own powers and destiny.

The **ENERGY FORMULA**, the **POWER OF GRATITUDE**, the **POWER OF SHARING**, the **POWER OF YES**, the **BELLYBUTTON**, all of those mindsets and recipe allowed me to become who I am today, and I am still just scratching the surface…

I achieved much and within record time, but until I put my bellybutton aside, I was still an **ARROGANT** limited by my own boundaries.

> "The day I looked up and left my bellybutton behind, that day I merged with the Universe."
> Dr. Bak Nguyen

By taking care of the needs of others, by sharing my experience and knowledge to empower, **arrogance became confidence**. That's how I started to change the world, with as least resistance as possible.

I am still naive, thinking that if I am working for the greater good, all will love and help me. Well, I like to think as such, but I also know too much to have expectations. I will hope, I will believe, and I will bet on myself to make it happen.

"Make it happen!"
Dr. Bak Nguyen

That was the signature phrase of **CHANGING THE WORLD FROM A DENTAL CHAIR**. Can you believe that while I am doing so, I am scoring a new world record monthly, every time that I am finishing a new book, which is twice a month?

Call me **ALPHA**, call me Doctor, call me wannabe, call me arrogant, it really does not matter anymore. Labels are labels, but my story, my legacy, my philosophy, those are things that will outlast the rumors, the glory, and the jealousy.

I have too much to accomplish and to discover to gate my heart or to close my mind. Once, I was asked in an interview what is a Momentum. Well, that took me a minute before I could formulate my answer as such:

> "A Momentum is when it is easier
> to keep moving than to stop."
> Dr. Bak Nguyen

Well, I believe that it is the same with the **POWER OF OPENNESS**. Eventually, you'll grow used to breathe the air and to see the light, wide open. Close the blinds, and you will suffer from depression. Leave the doors and the windows open for a while, and you will never want to close them back ever again.

After 18 months of saying **YES** to everything, I was a changed man, a very different man. Even if it wasn't all good, I didn't want to go back to my old self, it simply wasn't enough anymore. So I kept the doors open… well, the doors were gone!

If I was little before, today, I am a little bigger. I am more. I like to think that I am still little because there is so much more to discover and to master.

In other words, there are still so many mistakes to be made. The only question is: do I have a mind large enough to embrace them all?

> "Smaller the minds, lesser the mistakes…"
> Dr. Bak Nguyen

Yes, it is true, the smaller the mind, the fewer, the mistakes. But what fun will be left? Little, I like, small, I run from! With that mindset, it is simply crazy the immensity of **Abundance** that you will find.

Violence, fighting, cruelty, those are all children of **Scarcity**. Embrace **Abundance** once, and you will understand why there is nothing of worth for you in the smallness, any smallness.

No, this is not a lecture, it is not my place to lecture anyone. This is your hope that better and more exist and are within reach. I merged my own life experience with the journey on the other side to reassure you that it might be unknown, but there is no need to fear. It might not be easy, but the hardest, you are living it right now, each day, day after day.

Open up your mind and your heart,
Clemency will help you heal,
Candor will keep your hope up,
Playfulness will keep you moving forward.

This is what I've discovered, on the other side! Today, I am whole, and I am happy! Not content, happy! Since it is fun, well, I don't see any reason to stop or to slow down. Get rid of **Scarcity** and its derivatives, and **Abundance** is within your grasp.

More than once, you read in the previous chapter that the day you look up and see the horizon, really see the horizon, well, you also inherited the power of the Universe.

Well, that's what I mean, to drop **Scarcity** and **Smallness** behind to open up and embrace **Abundance** instead.

In medicine, we like to purge the body from time to time. It is called to cleanse our bodies. Well, drop **Scarcity**, and you will have purged most of your wounds and limitations.

Yes, Scarcity is just a sophisticated word to point at your fears. Shake them away, let go of your roots to free your legs and wings. Don't force your loved ones and peers, and mind your own liberation, your own ascension.

Behind you, paint the **HAPPY PLACES** to those you love, polish and share the tools you no longer need, that's your way to help, to be kind. Every time that you are giving back, you a growing a little more.

For those of you who are studying Maslow, what do we have at the top of the pyramid of needs? **SELF-ACTUALIZATION**, to achieve one's potential. Well, the way to do so is to give back.

> "The more you'll give, the more you'll grow!
> That's the equation of Abundance!"
> Dr. Bak Nguyen

I learnt a long time ago to keep my distance from those words, since they share the same roots as Scarcity.

Get rid of Scarcity
And most of your problems and vices are gone!
Fear, jealousy even violence,
Won't have any roots left to haunt us.

Amongst all the recipes and formulas,
This is the most important one,
Embrace Abundance

You will grow, you will heal,
You will be bigger, smarter, better.
But above everything else,
You will be happier.

> "Scarcity is the root of most of our flaws, even violence."
> Dr. Bak Nguyen

I shared with you my journey, my feeling, and the map I have from the **ALPHA JOURNEY**. It should ease your way and prepare you for what's to come. Don't limit yourself to what I shared, this is only my experience and how I got there.

If I have learnt one thing is that there are multiple realities to the same truth. Trust in yours, believes in yours, embrace yours. The mindsets will help, but adapt them as you see fit.

By the next time we meet, you'll be the one sharing, and I'll be the one listening.

Welcome to the Alphas. This is **AMONGST THE ALPHAS vol. 2 - On the other side.**

Dr. BAK NGUYEN

CHAPTER 8
"HUMILITY"
BY DR. BAK NGUYEN

Now you know what's on the other side. I could keep going and share with you the next steps, but where would be the fun in that? Your **ALPHA JOURNEY** is about walking and doing, not reading and talking. So do, go on and enjoy the ride, your ride!

I will still leave you with one last piece of advice, one that will propel you into orbit. You see, you can spend your entire life to become a champion. You can train your whole life to be a hero, but life does not end right after. So what then? What happens as the curtains close on you?

The champions, the heroes, they are **ALPHAS**. Eventually, all Alphas will become has-beens. Trust me, that's not an easy thing to take in.

I am still an **ALPHA** in my prime. I met and learnt from great people who were, not too long ago. It is not the greatest of feelings to remember what we've done once.

All of their lives, they ran forward and never looked back. They learnt to project themselves into the future and to master the present, that's how they built bridges between societies, generations, and worlds.

Some, like me, had to heal from their past first. Those who did, started a little later their journey. Were they stronger? Were they smarter? They survived and made peace with their past, we all did, to become Alphas.

> "We all, somehow, learnt to leave our past behind, not to turn into statues of salt."
> Dr. Bak Nguyen

Sure, they can become mentors and find synergy grooming a younger **ALPHA**, but nothing beats the real thing, that feeling of air on your face as you are running fast and scoring big!

I also met and learnt from mentors who are still very active. Strangely, they are still in ascension, rising within a new journey. The color of one's hair is not linked to the age of one's heart, that I can tell you. Those people were once leaders and heads of their respective industries, and they retired.

They couldn't stay still at home, so they went back out, in a different field. They have their contacts, their experience, their resources, and they are betting on themselves to keep changing the world, to yet learn something new, to win again, big!

One of them told me that he couldn't just stay home, comfortable with his millions, so he went out. Then, he was tired to always talk in the past tense… "It is too depressing to use verbs in the past tense continuously…" So he switches back to the present and future tense, that's how he became happy again!

Exchanging with him, I understood those tales of great warriors who said that the best death is an honourable one on the battlefield. Common sense will tell us to stay away from harm's way once we are out. That's not an Alpha speaking.

Being an Alpha is a choice, not a status. Trust me, nothing is more painful than not be able to do something we once mastered. Most Alphas didn't just master, they also mattered. To get over that is cruel!

You want proof, look at all those hanging on to power, even if they have long passed their time… Leadership is not something that lasts forever. It would be wise to remember that one.

> "Dragons are invisible because as they mastered a shape, they unlearn it to master a new one."
> Dr. Bak Nguyen & William Bak
> (From the Legend of the Dragon Heart)

This is what I wrote with William for our 3rd book together, **THE LEGEND OF THE DRAGON HEART**. If you think that dragons and Alphas are the same, to avoid the fate of becoming a **has-been**, an Alpha will have to unlearn to learn again, differently. That's how he or she will keep his relevancy.

In history, Micheal Jordan did that when he left the basketball game to embrace baseball. His stardom might still be basketball, but he was happy, rising up as a baseball athlete. He wasn't a has-been. He became a model and a legend.

Don't get me wrong, he was already a legend, but by doing it again, he became a symbol of the strength of **WILL** leading to flexibility and adaptation. That's how we've evolved as a species, from our ability to adapt. Micheal Jordan tapped right into our biggest asset and leveraged it into a living legend!

Steve Job held on to PIXAR because it would have been too embarrassing to fail again (in his own words). A few years later, PIXAR made him into a multi-billionaire, almost overnight as PIXAR's IPO was launched a few days after the opening of TOY STORY 2.

And that is only a part of his story, his second coming at Apple made him into a legend and a pop culture figure. The day he came back to Apple, his old mentor, and now adversary, told him that he has to reinvent himself. He took the advice and did exactly that, he reinvented himself and Apple Computer with it.

Less than a decade after he took back the reins of APPLE, well they decided to drop the COMPUTER from the name of the company. They did so because even if the APPLE computer market shares were souring, they were counting for about 25% of the business of APPLE INC.

Within a decade, the company, under the leadership of Steve Job, captured the imagination of the world with new and innovative solutions. They were both creative and flexible in their approach.

Steve Job became a legend, not only to the tekkies and the financial world but to all artists, entrepreneurs, and dreamers, aspiring for more, for better. He proved the power of the mind over the odds.

Those great minds refused to throw down the towel after the fame and success. Well, they did so because they kept their heart young, believing in the future, despite their past.

When you think of it, it is exactly what every one of us should be doing: to believe in our future, despite our past, whatever our past is.

To the kids, the dragons have to master an emotion to master a shape. Then, to keep the fun going, they have to unlearn what they learnt to learn a new shape, a new emotion. The unlearning part is very important here since no two emotions are the same.

Just like mastering a new discipline, one cannot expect to keep doing what served him great once and think that it will be working again as well. Don't forget that the real goal wasn't the result, but the learning process!

"To keep learning, that's the youth, that's the power!"
Dr. Bak Nguyen

So dragons unlearn to free their mind completely before they start learning something new. That's what Alphas who want to avoid the has-been stage should do too, to stay humble and to keep learning, until their next phase, to unlearn and learn something new.

Very few Alphas will be able to leave their medals and achievements on their pinnacle of fame and success. It is not an easy choice to make, to walk away and keep pushing, but those are the **joy of youth** and the **magic of abundance**.

Remember the **Energy Formula**? The total Energy available is divided by the values one holds. Well, medals and past achievements are pretty heavy values.

To illustrate that last point, Micheal Phelps is the world's most medalled person in the history of mankind. Did you ever see Micheal swim with his medals around his neck? You get the point.

"Being an Alpha is not to be the first, but to keep being. By being, I meant learning and doing."
Dr. Bak Nguyen

Both the learning and doing are important to constitute the presence of an Alpha. And how can one keep learning, even at the top of his or her field?

Well, for centuries, people are looking for ways to stay forever young. **Humility** is what you seek.

We started this book as **ALPHAS**, what a bold statement! Actually, it was an affirmation of our freewill to embrace our **ALPHA GENE**. It had to be a clean and clear statement.

Then, we learnt not to depend on others to keep ourselves moving. We learnt not to define ourselves with anything but our thoughts and results. People called us arrogant at some point. And we kept building, with confidence!

Bold, arrogant, confident, determinate, those are all compatible with Humility! No matter where you stand, **Humility** is what will keep you young, and ready for more, for new.

> "You wanted to live forever. Well, stay humble!"
> Dr. Bak Nguyen

Humility is not to silence what you know and who you are, but to recognize what you don't know and who you are not, yet! Only humble can you keep learning, and unlearning. And what does being humble really mean? It means to keep our mind open, just like being generous will keep our heart open.

And once again, the magic of the Universe will operate on you. Have you ever loved? Those who had, all know that the more love you give, the more you will receive. Well, what works like a charm with **Generosity** also works with **Humility**… with a little twist.

The more you'll learn, the less you know, that's what it means to be humble. But at least now, you know. And if you must know, that's the difference between being smart and being wise.

> "Be bold, confident, and humble."
> Dr. Bak Nguyen

For those of you with more interest in the power of Humility, I've dedicated my 50th book on the matter, **HUMILITY FOR SUCCESS**. Again, another recipe to keep scoring, to keep learning, and to stay young forever!

I can only speak for myself here, but I know for a fact that my worse punishment will be to sit on my lap to enjoy my glory. Sure I am lazy, and I am looking to score, big. But, my real fun is to do that again, faster, bigger and in a different field.

I went from dentistry to finance, reshaping part of the world to address the inefficiencies. I went from finance to writing, sharing with you the journey and the motivation. The only things that I kept from one field to the next are my integrity and my will to adapt… and to forge.

Just like one has to learn to build before he could learn to destroy, I had to learn to adapt before I could forge things that would outlast my existence. And the only way is with respect, **Generosity**, and **flexibility**. In a word, **Humility**.

This is my last chapter within the second volume of **AMONGST THE ALPHAS**, I am not sure if there will be a third volume. If I started this journey with hesitation, I learned so much on the way. Now I know that this is amongst my **MUST READ BOOK**.

From one chapter to the next, I had the chance to make sense of my own journey, of what really happened, of why, and how it happened. Today I brought you the hope that everyone is free to become an Alpha, that everyone can be an Alpha. You just have to embrace that half of yourself, of your **ALPHA GENE**.

Embrace your **ALPHA GENE**
To be greater than yourself
Embrace your **ALPHA GENE**
To do more than you ever imagined

Embrace your **ALPHA GENE**
This is how you will reach
Your Destiny

Your Destiny, this is not a word for the books or legend, it is what you've been looking for, your entire life. Only once you are ready, can you start that journey.

The **Quest of Identity**, that's everyone's journey and the first one that will matter. Will that journey be about healing, about accepting, about rising? We each have our unique challenges.

Sooner or later, every one of us without exception will take the trip to find out who he or she really is. To open that question is to ask questions about all of our being. The only variables are how soon will you be answering your interrogations and how long will you have to walk in **YOUR NEW SHOES**.

Well, I can't rush you on that. Bringing the **ALPHA** alternative to the table is my way to give you leverage to pace up your walk and discoveries. Even your **Destiny** might take a new turn with the **ALPHA GENE** in the equation.

It is a choice. It is your choice.

Welcome to the Alphas. This is **AMONGST THE ALPHAS vol. 2 - On the other side.**

Dr. BAK NGUYEN

PART II
BY GUEST AUTHORS

CHAPTER 9
"THE ALPHAS TRAITS"
BY DR. LINA DUSEVIČIŪTĖ

When Dr. Bak first invited me to join this Alpha journey, writing about being an alpha, immediately, I said yes! I said yes, because I appreciate him and what he does immensely. Also, his story and emotional journey are very relatable to me. Nevertheless, I was rather surprised because I've never thought about myself as an alpha before.

However, the perspective of the surrounding world may give us a lot of insights. I decided to give it a thought, it is always worth investigating to see how others see us. There is also one important aspect of how our brain works:

"We can only perceive things that we can distinguish."
Dr. Lina Dusevičiūtė

So when you become familiar, with distinction you can understand the world or your personality more clearly. This also enables us to operate and act from that distinction. It becomes real, and shifts our world.

For example, in the Russian language, there is no word for security. Therefore as a distinction, there is no such thing as security. I'm not the best politician but I will dare to propose a hypothesis that in Russia, people do not feel as safe. It is the same as that you couldn't see the colour blue if you wouldn't know how to name it. But that's only a hypothesis.

I would love to be seen, to see myself and to feel as an Alpha. While writing this chapter, I tried to see the world through *Alpha glasses*, and to see myself as one.

Since Dr. Bak encouraged me to think about and to consider what it is to be an Alpha and what is it means, few things became clear to me.

First of all, you are not born Alpha, you choose to be one. Each one of us is free to choose to be and to become, or not. Secondly, being an Alpha is not an easy choice nor a comfortable choice. Nonetheless, it is truly an empowering one.

In my views, being an Alpha includes few key aspects. I would consider one of the main traits of an alpha personality type is to **take responsibility for more than just yourself**. The roots of this responsibility need to come, not from wanting to control others, so that the world would go in your way, but from caring for others.

> "Caring for the world and the fate of others is truly possible just when one sees how we are all intertwined, entangled, and connected."
> Dr. Lina Dusevičiūtė

The current situation about the COVID vaccine gives a great opportunity to illustrate that. Amongst my colleagues, there were some doubts of whether to take the vaccine or not. I would lie if I were to say that I hadn't thought twice before accepting the vaccine. I did. I decided to get vaccinated, not only because I was convinced that it's good for me, and that the vaccine is reliable enough, but because I felt a responsibility to the world, to the people under my care.

I've asked myself a question, that I carried to my colleagues as well: take your point of view, your attitude and apply it to each and every person on the planet, and then, ask yourself would you like to live in that same world?

> "Make sure that your approach, attitude, and decisions, when applied to each and every person in the world, would make a better picture than the currently existing one."
> Dr. Lina Dusevičiūtė

And this leads us to the other aspect of being an Alpha. It's the **courage to speak your mind** and what you stand for. Even if your position will be uncomfortable, perhaps, even unpopular. I will be bold enough to propose that Alphas have a big part of *stoicism* in them.

One of the earlier stoics, Cato, use to purposefully wear miss-matched clothing in the high-profile arenas and be teased or smirked at, to train himself to be only ashamed of the things worth being ashamed for.

I also like to test my resilience in doing something unpopular or disobeying a dress code. I've tried that exercise. My aim was to conquer the feeling of **not fitting in**. I wanted to feel free and good, despite being an ugly duck amongst the swans.

Basically, I just repeated the Cato's recipe. Let me reveal a secret. I enjoyed it! My comfort zone expanded so much from this experiment. It is a great way to grow your resilience.

I will state that Alphas usually are hard workers. They don't shy away from difficult steps, obstacles, and challenges. When they believe the path they are on, they thrive walking, trying and learning.

Sometimes this may lead to flirt with dangerous lines and boundaries as an Alpha is so driven, stubborn, or determined. In those cases, some may even damage themselves. This happened to me.

I got so stubborn, worked so many hours, had huge expectations for myself that I burnt myself out. I was working 12 hours a day, six days a week. I used to run 8 to 10 km 6 times a week. Do I even need to mention that I had almost no social life?

I didn't sleep much, didn't eat much either. I just couldn't stop. Going on this pace was bad but stopping felt even worse. It took me a year to recover. I still love to immerse myself in work and creative activities, but what I've learnt is to let go.

To let go of the *grip of expectations*, of control. I learnt to be aware and sensitive to myself and to the world in *present tense*. I realized that I am an instrument for myself to experience the flavours of life.

I learnt to treat myself with more consideration. Out of this comes an another Alpha trait: to **seek an advantage out of every situation**, which means to learn the lessons that Life teaches us. If something seemingly bad happens, I immediately say to myself what is the *"advantage"?* I need to find something positive in each situation, something advantageous that I can leverage on. Today, it has become a reflex.

People usually enjoy your company. They enjoy feeling a strong frame, they can the confidence that someone knows what *he's doing, speaking, where he's going*. They enjoyed the assurance, courage, inspiration, optimism, and energy that you radiate. It is contagious . You are an Alpha.

After spending some time with an Alpha, people surrounding them are elevated by osmosis, just by sharing their vibe and presence. This is only possible when you are, yourself, strong and confident. When you are both physically and mentally in a *power position*, an *alpha position*.

I believe that it's a responsibility, once you chose to be an Alpha, a leader, to take care of yourself first because only then, can you provide the benefits of your energy to others. That is why to me, being alone for some time is crucial. Even though I love people, love serving them, I always find time to spend just by myself, for myself.

> "To be alone, that is the secret of invention; to be alone, that is when ideas are born."
> Nikola Tesla

I agree with him. And I will add, it is a pause when you take time to inhale. How long can you survive when you're just exhaling, exhaling, and keep exhaling... So I stopped and took a deep breath. Then I chose to be an Alpha, because I care, and this is my way to be of service to the world.

My name is Dr. Lina Dusevičiūtė and I am an Alpha.

Welcome to the Alphas. This is **AMONGST THE ALPHAS vol. 2 - On the other side.**

Dr. BAK NGUYEN

CHAPTER 10
"I AM AN ALPHA"
BY DR. DUC-MINH LAM-DO

My name is Dr. Duc-Minh Lam-Do. I am a very practical man. I love actions more than words. In here, I will share with you the facts and actions that led the way to my journey as an Alpha.

When I first met Dr. Bak a few years ago, we casually spoke about the topics of dentistry that fuelled us, and then came the topic of the Alphas. I always wondered about that group of individuals whom he referred to once in a while.

We met again, and again, and fast-forward a few phone calls and Zoom calls later, he welcomed me in the **Alphas**. I was surprised and somewhat speechless as I did not fully grasp what this group was about and needed more details. And so Dr. Bak explained to me how he came up with that name, what the individuals who were part of it were about, but mostly he emphasized what an "Alpha" embodies.

That meeting we had was a few weeks after the March 16th, 2020 lockdown for our dental offices that the Quebec Public Health ordered. It was in the midst of the pandemic that we are still living as I write these lines.

I am just a regular general dentist who is passionate about his profession and who happens to care a lot about his patients' wellbeing. Since we could no longer see them in clinic, we had to find a way to reach out to them and for them, to reach out to us, for whatever reasons or concerns that they had about their oral health.

I took it on my shoulders that all my patients can rely on me whenever in need and I consider myself to have a very close relationship with my patients, a relationship that is earned and that I do not take for granted.

A solution had to come quickly to face the months we had ahead of us. That solution took shape in: "**Télédentistes**", a dental telemedicine platform that allowed the population in Quebec to seek the help of a dental professional from the comfort of their own home whenever and wherever, as long as there was an internet connection. It was up and running in mid-April and that caught the attention of Dr. Bak.

We spoke a lot, exchanged ideas, participated in virtual Summits, and met dentists from around the Globe who were going through the same issues worldwide. We refused to let our patients be on their own with their pain and oral conditions, we all wanted to contribute and help them the best we could because in 2020, it just did not make sense that they had to suffer and wait to be seen in a clinical setting.

I guess that's a bit what being an Alpha meant to me. To refuse the status quo, to refuse to be beaten by this pandemic, and to always strive to do better to serve the population, the patients who rely so heavily on us.

Being proactive when facing a situation is the surest way to conquer it. This was no exception. It was unacceptable that our patients who allow us the privilege to serve them be left alone.

We channeled that frustration to put up **Télédentistes**, the first teledentistry platform in Quebec.

So if that's what it took to "*become*" an **Alpha**, then I believe we can all become Alphas, all of us who want more out of life, who want something better for our society, all of us whose creativity and vision will dictate and shape our industry in the years to come.

It all starts with an idea. It is then up to us to take that idea to fruition or to surround ourselves with experts who can help us make that idea happen.

> "At the core of it, I think that being an Alpha is about accepting the responsibility to be a leader in our profession."
> Dr. Duc-Minh Lam-Do

Being an Alpha is about wanting to redefine the standards of practice in our industry. Excellence is not an option, it has to be the end result: excellence in service, excellence in care delivery, and always to surpass patients' expectations.

Sometimes, life throws a curveball at you. That's what COVID-19 did to our industry. But it's how we deal with that curveball that defines us. Being on the sidelines was not an option for us. Even though we had countless sleepless nights, we overworked at a time when most the world had their spirits down with uncertainty, but the reward was so gratifying at the end, it was worth all the effort and sweat.

Being an Alpha also involves: rising in times of doubt and stepping up for our colleagues, our peers, our patients who depend on us, and encouraging others around you to do the same.

Even though you become part of that group of individuals, nothing should be ever taken for granted. I strongly believe all of us should constantly be on the lookout to better our protocols, to better our systems, and to reflect on ways to better serve the person who entitles us to our job: the patient.

> "The alpha journey is an insatiable quest to become a better professional, a leader in our profession and community, and to find ways to deal with different circumstances of life."
> Dr. Duc-Minh Lam-Do

Because at the end of the tunnel lies your real purpose and you cannot grasp it until your vision aligns with it. And if being an Alpha is part of the equation, I'm honoured to take on such a role.

My name is Dr. Duc-Minh Lam-Do and I am an Alpha.

Welcome to the Alphas. This is **AMONGST THE ALPHAS vol. 2 - On the other side.**

Dr. BAK NGUYEN

CHAPTER 11
"LIVING THE CHANGE"
BY DR. JULIO REYNAFARJE

It is incredible how in a year our lives changed remarkably. Since this pandemic was declared, our job change, most of the time we usually take care of our patients (who are always our priority), and many of us not only dedicate ourselves to them, we shared our spare time between classrooms and family. That day suddenly, our way of life stop and the confinement time began.

We had to temporarily close our offices. The classes we teach to our students are now theoretical and virtual, and it led us to do a bigger effort to keep working with our patients and students, leading us to improve and be more human at each and every encounter.

Despite that, and for good, we also shared more time with our families. The fraternal bond became stronger, and this interaction made our natural instinct to help people lead us to reinvent ourselves, to generate new resources and to reach more people.

Today our life is changing, our way of socializing begins with a meeting with zoom. Before, this was very distant and rare, almost alien. Today it is a very common way to keep in touch with our colleagues and friends.

The conversations today are deeper than before, our concerns are different, and we discovered that we are happy with simpler things. Today we value watching a sunset, breathing fresh air in the morning, or enjoying a starry sky, a couple of years ago, we restricted these pleasures to our vacation trips.

All change is good, particularly this pandemic divided this last year into several stages of evolution, which I am going to describe in this little story.

The first days were confusing, spending many hours at home, without much to do, without knowing how to react to a dark cloud that could arrive at any time and that we did not have the possibility to understand how it affects us. We had to make decisions and see the best way to take advantage of all that free time at the moment we were living.

As this epidemic began to grow, we had to make decisions about how we should use our time in the best way. We were getting more and more used to confinement and the hours were getting longer every day. I realized that we are having a lot of time to think and be active In the way of reversing the situation we were going through.

Many people began to inform themselves and start to learn about this pandemic, so I also joined the trend. First studying how new research trends were discovering the modus operandi of this hidden enemy, and this knowledge led me to have respect for the disease, not fear as Dr. Eric Pulver, a fellow Alpha, once told me.

This curiosity also began to grow in fields in which we were more comfortable. In our case, looking for a way to improve our way of treating Dental patients in a safe and practical manner, ideas such as personal protection systems for both patients and doctors were born. These systems had to be ergonomic and adapted to our offices as well.

In my case, my mind started to fly a little bit more out of the box. I created an air mask using no fabrics, do transparent isolation box systems. I've also developed protocols for recording vital signs for all patients before they enter the office and many more. I realized that innovation and entrepreneurship began to take a more important role in my everyday work.

At that time a message appeared on my professional social network (Linkedin), with an invitation to talk about how this pandemic had affected the professionals in my country. Usually, I upload original articles about my personal professional experience with an alternative educational vision. These called the Attention from a Doctor in Canada with an impressive record of entrepreneurship.

If there is something that I will always appreciate all of my life, it is that invitation from my friend Dr. Bak Nguyen. It is incredible how this friendly meeting opened my world to meet so many interesting Alphas and doctors with a vision of life similar to mine.

The moment of the explosion has arrived, new projects began to grow every day. Dr. Bak, world record author, invited me to write a few chapters in his books. Soon, we co-signed a book together, **MIDAS TOUCH,** addressing the need of a human touch in the approach of our medical duty. MIDAS TOUCH is today available on most platforms, namely, APPLE BOOKS, KINDLE, AMAZON print on demand and even BARNES & NOBLE. Meeting with Dr. Bak opened a whole new world of possibilities.

I started developing entrepreneurial projects, and now, all this new experience during the pandemic led me to have an impressive social network with experts from all over the world.

Today I exchange with Alphas from Canada, Spain, United States, Lithuania, Slovenia, India, Switzerland, Bulgaria, Malaysia, Greece and many other places that make the world increasingly integrated and smaller, all with a common goal: to improve and make a better world for our patients.

This pandemic has made us aware of how fragile we are, our mortality. It has affected us all in different ways. We all know people who left us or have been affected due to this virus, in my personal experience I lost family, friends, and today they are memories and example that drive us to continue fighting for those who come after us.

Today we are experiencing change, constant growth and development are part of our life, but also we learn how to have a more noble and human vision because today our concern is to improve the world and the lives of the people we serve and love. To me, that's what Alphas do.

My name is Dr. Julio Reynafarje and I am an Alpha.

Welcome to the Alphas. This is **AMONGST THE ALPHAS vol. 2 - On the other side.**

Dr. BAK NGUYEN

CONCLUSION
BY DR. BAK NGUYEN

Wow, I don't know about you but as for me, I need to take a pause and to breathe. If going through **AMONGST THE ALPHAS** vol. 1 was a breeze, vol. 2 proved to be much harder. Why? Because now, we have to walk our talk.

What I shared with you in this journey, I walked through each moment and I am still carrying the scars on my back. But I also healed from my past and legacy. Where my wings were amputated, I found new ways to fly, even higher.

> "The hope of an Alpha is within the beliefs that healing is possible."
> Dr. Bak Nguyen

That said, to become an Alpha, we must have first, the desire to heal ourselves. In other words, we must want and accept to change. With that change come the consequences of our choices and actions. Losing your friends and part of your family is the most painful of the challenges.

> "But as I came to understand, it is either to lose them or to lose yourself!"
> Dr. Bak Nguyen

Some will argue that it is self-preservation that brought us to break the chains. Some will even qualify as ungrateful and selfish our decisions and actions to break free. Well, ever heard the saying that "Misery loves company?"

As I learnt the hard way to respect the choice of each person, I must also have the courage to respect myself, to listen to that inner voice whispering. It was whispering at first, trying to find a voice through the noise and the barking.

As one learns to recognize his or her voice, it will feel natural, just as a new born recognizes the voice of his mother. Slowly that voice will raise and elevate to resonate with your entire body, making you feel whole for the first time. Just like sex, it will be a moment of climax.

Just like sex, it does not have to be a unique experience, a once-in-a-lifetime thing! It does not even have to be exclusive. That's against the **Law of Abundance**. So once you feel whole, you can make the choice to come back to what you knew but, once again, you are screwed. You will never forget that feeling of being whole, of resonating at the frequency of the Universe. And that's is what being an Alpha is all about, about being one with the Universe.

Why do you think that being humble, generous and caring are trades of Alphas? Because those lead to the pillar frequencies of the Universe. Give and feel the power. Share and feel the growth.

> "Growth happens at the giving end,
> not the receiving one."
> Dr. Bak Nguyen

You must be humble enough to ask when you are in need or are lacking. You must be humble to accept and to learn. For that, be grateful and remember what you received, learnt and who gave to you. Now that you've grown, you must give back tenfold.

Is that a bad bargain? What do we know about growing? It happens as we give. So the more you have to give, the more you will grow. Can you find a better bargain?

> "Give and grow. I never said sacrifice."
> Dr. Bak Nguyen

To sacrifice is to cut a vital part away, thinking that it is giving. Well, if some situations will push a loving one to the ultimate decision of sacrifice, most of Life does not have to be as dramatic. Resonate with the frequencies of the Universe, close your eyes and see what's ahead.

Once you have the **clarity of the Universe**, you can read the future, at least part of it. But most importantly, you can see people for who they really are. Turn a blind eye to that truth, you may not live to retell the story…

> "Be generous, grateful, and genuine, not naive."
> Dr. Bak Nguyen

Doing so, because you care for more than yourself, you will learn quickly to find, even to create, more and more resources. Welcome the help, but don't expect everyone to be like you. If you ask me, don't even expect people to be grateful. That part is their own journey and burden to walk, not yours. Be, give, and move on, you are growing and flying away.

In the process, you must also learn to respect the freedom and beliefs of everyone. Don't try to force freedom or to free someone without their consent. There is no love or joy there, just pain, sorrow, and even more pain!

As Alphas, our role is not to be the heroes, but to be ready and present as Destiny calls. When the needs and the challenges will arise, we will be there to respond. Before that point, all we did was to free ourselves and to train to open up and to adapt, as quickly as possible. And that's the expression of the **ALPHA GENE**.

> "To empower is not to give power but to help one discover his or her own powers within."
> Dr. Bak Nguyen

And this is why and how, amongst Alphas, we are not killing each other. Alphas are not playing the **king of the hill** game, that's for the beta, delta, and others… Being the *king of the hill* will ground your frequency to the hill.

An Alpha, even as he or his is climbing a mountain, he is just passing through. What he or she is keeping is the experience of the journey, not the mountain itself. Imagine a *hill*?

If in the first volume of **AMONGST THE ALPHAS**, I encouraged you to find your voice and to start your journey, in the second volume, I shared genuinely with you with candor and without filters, the challenges and pains ahead. I wish that I knew a better way but I don't. What **Conformity** did, it is now for us to undo, one by one.

Actually, that was a lie. There is a better way. Not for us. For us, it is too late and we must undo to heal but for our children, we can save them the pain of **Conformity** before its *blades* touch our children.

That love is what elevates me to rise up, the love for my child. I did not want him to suffer as I did. I did not want my son to hate me because I wanted what I thought was good for him. I did not want my kid to be torn between being loyal, grateful, and free. Because of that, I got rid of the doubts and walked my way to undo and heal.

I healed quickly because it wasn't about me, I still need to parve the way to my son, before the **blades of Conformity** could get anywhere near him. I undid, healed, and evolved. Then, I became strong enough to save my son from most of the pain and amputations of **Conformity**.

Today, he does not need to heal, just to discover himself with confidence and to try his God-given powers, without doubt, and second thoughts.

> "I found my Alpha powers through love, without sacrifices."
> Dr. Bak Nguyen

And that's the mindset and state of mind he inherited from me. But it does not have to be exclusively within parenting. That mindset can be applied anywhere and in most situations. This is how my Alpha colleagues joined me with their unique stories.

Lina, Duc, and Julio are from different continents, from different generations and yet, they share a common desire and story. They all grew, helping others. As I asked them to join, they never hesitated because the vibe was familiar. We were all connected from the frequencies of the Universe.

Then, as I invited them to join my writing to share their perspective, they might have used different labels but in the end, it was the same story. They would have walked their journey no matter what. They would have because it is in their nature. Regrouping and sharing amongst Alphas simply made it easier and incorporate the fun factor in.

You too, you don't have to stand alone to prove a point. After the rejection and the reboot of your values and system, you are an Alpha. That was your first choice. Now, your second choice is whether or not to stand amongst Alphas.

And remember, as you stand amongst Alphas, you are there to give, not to take. Empower others and you will grow beyond your understanding. Can you feel the release of energy already? Now, what do you think happens when each of the Alpha is releasing as much energy? Well, they grow, riding the **forces of Abundance!**

My name is Dr. Bak and I am an Alpha standing amongst Alphas.

Welcome to the Alphas. This is **AMONGST THE ALPHAS vol. 2 - On the other side.**

Dr. BAK NGUYEN

ABOUT THE AUTHORS

From Canada, **Dr BAK NGUYEN**, Nominee Ernst and Young Entrepreneur of the year, Grand Homage Lys DIVERSITY, and LinkedIn & TownHall Achiever of the year. Dr Bak is a cosmetic dentist, CEO and founder of Mdex & Co. His company is revolutionizing the dental field. Speaker and motivator, he wrote 72 books over 36 months accumulating many world records (to be officialized).

- ENTREPRENEURSHIP
- LEADERSHIP
- QUEST OF IDENTITY
- DENTISTRY AND MEDICINE
- PARENTING
- CHILDREN BOOKS
- PHILOSOPHY

In 2003, he founded Mdex, a dental company upon which in 2018, he launched the most ambitious private endeavour to reform the dental industry, Canada wide. Philosopher, he has close to his heart the quest of happiness of the people surrounding him, patients and colleagues alike. In 2020, he launched an International collaborative initiative named **THE ALPHAS** to share knowledge and for Entrepreneurs and Doctors to thrive through the Greatest Pandemic and Economic depression of our time.

In 2016, he co-found with Tranie Vo, Emotive World Incorporated, a tech research company to use technology to empower happiness and sharing. U.A.X. the ultimate audio experience is the landmark project on which the team is advancing, utilizing the technics of the movie industry and the advancement in ARTIFICIAL INTELLIGENCE to save the book industry and to upgrade the continuing education space.

These projects have allowed Dr Nguyen to attract interests from the international and diplomatic community and he is now the center of a global discussion in the wellbeing and the future of the health profession. It is in that matter that he shares his thoughts and encourages the health community to share their own stories.

"It's not worth it go through it alone! Together, we stand, alone, we fall."

Motivational speaker and serial entrepreneur, philosopher and author, from his own words, Dr Nguyen describes himself as a dentist by circumstances, an entrepreneur by nature and a communicator by passion.

He also holds recognitions from the Canadian Parliament and the Canadian Senate

ABOUT THE GUEST AUTHORS

From USA, **Dr. Maria Kunstadter**, Doctor of Dental Surgery, co-founder THE TELEDENTIST, the biggest TELEDENTISTRY provider in USA. Experienced President with a demonstrated history of working in the hospital & health care industry. Skilled in Customer Service, Sales, Strategic Planning, Team Building, and Public Speaking. Strong business development professional with a Doctor of Dental Surgery focused in Advanced General Dentistry from UMKC School of Dentistry.

From USA: **Dr. Paul Ouellette**, DDS, MS, ABO, AFAAID, WORLD TOP 100 DENTISTS, Former Associate Professor Georgia School of Orthodontics and Jacksonville University. A visionary man looking for the future of our profession. Dr. Paul Ouellette Highly motivated to help my sons become successful in the "Ouellette Family of Dentists" Group Dental Specialty Practice.

From USA, **Dr. Jeremy Krell**, dentist MBA and serial entrepreneur, the real definition of an OVERACHIEVER. Highly experienced innovator and entrepreneur with a proven track record of taking early-stage startups to acquisition (multi-million dollar buyout). Excellent clinical dentistry and communication skills with in-depth analytical, organizational, and problem-solving abilities. A detail orientated and strategic leader in a dynamic, expeditious innovative environment. Firm experience with strategy, positioning companies, leading & developing teams, raising capital, investor relations, dental materials & techniques, negotiating & closing deals, and sales.

www.DrBakNguyen.com

ULTIMATE AUDIO EXPERIENCE

A new way to learn and enjoy Audiobooks. Made to be entertaining while keeping the self-educational value of a book, UAX will appeal to both auditive and visual people. UAX is the blockbuster of the Audiobooks.

UAX will cover most of Dr Bak's books, and is now negotiating to bring more authors and more titles to the UAX concept. Now streaming on Spotify, Apple Music and available for download on all major music platforms. Give it a try today!

AMAZON - BARNES & NOBLE - APPLE BOOKS - KINDLE
SPOTIFY - APPLE MUSIC

COMBO
PAPERBACK/AUDIOBOOK
ACTIVATION

Please register your book to receive the link to your audiobook version. Register at:
https://baknguyen.com/amongst-the-alphas-2-registry

Your license of the audiobook allows you to share with up to 3 peoples the audiobook contained at this link. Book published by Dr. Bak publishing company. Audiobook produced by Emotive World Inc. Copyright 2021, All right reserved.

FROM THE SAME AUTHOR
Dr Bak Nguyen

www.DrBakNguyen.com

FACTEUR HUMAIN -035
LE LEADERSHIP DU SUCCÈS
par Dr. BAK NGUYEN & CHRISTIAN TRUDEAU

ehappyPedia -038
THE RISE OF THE UNICORN
BY Dr. BAK NGUYEN & Dr. JEAN DE SERRES

CHAMPION MINDSET -039
LEARNING TO WIN
BY Dr. BAK NGUYEN & CHRISTOPHE MULUMBA

THE RISE OF THE UNICORN 2 -076
eHappyPedia
BY Dr BAK NGUYEN & Dr JEAN DE SERRES

BRANDING DrBAK -044
BALANCING STRATEGY AND EMOTIONS
BY Dr. BAK NGUYEN

SYMPHONY OF SKILLS -001
BY Dr. BAK NGUYEN

002 - **La Symphonie des Sens**
ENTREPREUNARIAT
par Dr. BAK NGUYEN

006 - **Industries Disruptors**
BY Dr .BAK NGUYEN

007 - **Changing the World from a dental chair**
BY Dr. BAK NGUYEN

008 - **The Power Behind the Alpha**
BY TRANIE VO & Dr. BAK NGUYEN

036 - **SELFMADE**
GRATITUDE AND HUMILITY
BY Dr. BAK NGUYEN

072 - **THE U.A.X. STORY**
THE ULTIMATE AUDIO EXPERIENCE
BY Dr. BAK NGUYEN

088 - **CRYPTOCONOMICS 101**
MY PERSONAL JOURNEY FROM 50K TO 1 MILLION
BY Dr BAK NGUYEN

with William Bak

The Trilogy of Legends

THE LEGEND OF THE CHICKEN HEART -016
LA LÉGENDE DU COEUR DE POULET -017
BY Dr. BAK NGUYEN & WILLIAM BAK

THE LEGEND OF THE LION HEART -018
LA LÉGENDE DU COEUR DE LION -019
BY Dr. BAK NGUYEN & WILLIAM BAK

THE LEGEND OF THE DRAGON HEART -020
LA LÉGENDE DU COEUR DE DRAGON -021
BY Dr. BAK NGUYEN & WILLIAM BAK

WE ARE ALL DRAGONS -022
NOUS TOUS, DRAGONS -023
BY Dr. BAK NGUYEN & WILLIAM BAK

THE 9 SECRETS OF THE SMART CHICKEN -025
LES 9 SECRETS DU POULET INTELLIGENT -026
BY Dr. BAK NGUYEN & WILLIAM BAK

THE SECRET OF THE FAST CHICKEN -027
LE SECRETS DU POULET RAPIDE -028
BY Dr. BAK NGUYEN & WILLIAM BAK

THE LEGEND OF THE SUPER CHICKEN -029
LA LÉGENDE DU SUPER POULET -030
BY Dr. BAK NGUYEN & WILLIAM BAK

031- **THE STORY OF THE CHICKEN SHIT**
032- **L'HISTOIRE DU CACA DE POULET**
BY Dr. BAK NGUYEN & WILLIAM BAK

033- **WHY CHICKEN CAN'T DREAM?**
034- **POURQUOI LES POULETS NE RÊVENT PAS?**
BY Dr. BAK NGUYEN & WILLIAM BAK

057- **THE STORY OF THE CHICKEN NUGGET**
083- **HISTOIRE DE POULET: LA PÉPITE**
BY Dr. BAK NGUYEN & WILLIAM BAK

082- **CHICKEN FOREVER**
084- **POULET POUR TOUJOURS**
BY Dr BAK NGUYEN & WILLIAM BAK

THE SPIES AND ALIENS
COLLECTION

077- **THE VACCINE**
079- **LE VACCIN**
077B- **LA VACUNA**
BY Dr BAK NGUYEN & WILLIAM BAK
TRANSLATION BY BRENDA GARCIA

PROFESSION HEALTH - TOME ONE -005
THE UNCONVENTIONAL
QUEST OF HAPPINESS
BY Dr. BAK NGUYEN, Dr. MIRJANA SINDOLIC,
Dr. ROBERT DURAND AND COLLABORATORS

HOW TO NOT FAIL AS A DENTIST -047
BY Dr. BAK NGUYEN

SUCCESS IS A CHOICE -060
BLUEPRINTS FOR HEALTH
PROFESSIONALS
BY Dr. BAK NGUYEN

RELEVANCY - TOME TWO -064
REINVENTING OURSELVES TO SURVIVE
BY Dr. BAK NGUYEN & Dr. PAUL OUELLETTE AND
COLLABORATORS

MIDAS TOUCH -065
POST-COVID DENTISTRY
BY Dr. BAK NGUYEN, Dr. JULIO REYNAFARJE AND
Dr. PAUL OUELLETTE

THE POWER OF DR -066
THE MODERN TITLE OF NOBILITY
BY Dr. BAK NGUYEN, Dr. PAVEL KRASTEV AND
COLLABORATORS

004- **IDENTITY**
THE ANTHOLOGY OF QUESTS
BY Dr. BAK NGUYEN

011- **HYBRID**
THE MODERN QUEST OF IDENTITY
BY Dr. BAK NGUYEN

045- **HORIZON, BUILDING UP THE VISION**
VOLUME ONE
BY Dr. BAK NGUYEN

048- **HORIZON, ON THE FOOTSTEPS OF TITANS**
VOLUME TWO
BY Dr. BAK NGUYEN

068- **HORIZON, DREAMING OF TRAVELING**
VOLUME THREE
BY Dr. BAK NGUYEN

MOMENTUM TRANSFER -009
BY Dr. BAK NGUYEN & Coach DINO MASSON

LEVERAGE -014
COMMUNICATION INTO SUCCESS
BY Dr. BAK NGUYEN AND COLLABORATORS

**HOW TO WRITE A BOOK
IN 30 DAYS** -042
BY Dr. BAK NGUYEN

POWER -043
EMOTIONAL INTELLIGENCE
BY Dr. BAK NGUYEN

**HOW TO WRITE A SUCCESSFUL
BUSINESS PLAN** -049
BY Dr BAK NGUYEN & ROUBA SAKR

MINDSET ARMORY -050
BY Dr. BAK NGUYEN

**MASTERMIND, 7 WAYS INTO THE
BIG LEAGUE** -052
BY Dr. BAK NGUYEN & JONAS DIOP

PLAYBOOK INTRODUCTION -055
BY Dr. BAK NGUYEN

PLAYBOOK INTRODUCTION 2 -056
BY Dr. BAK NGUYEN

062- **RISING**
TO WIN MORE THAN
YOU ARE AFRAID TO LOSE
BY Dr. BAK NGUYEN

067- **TORNADO**
FORCE OF CHANGE
BY Dr. BAK NGUYEN

071- **BOOTCAMP**
BOOKS TO REWRITE MINDSETS
INTO WINNING STATES OF MIND
BY Dr. BAK NGUYEN

078- **POWERPLAY**
HOW TO BUILD THE PERFECT TEAM
BY Dr. BAK NGUYEN

024- **THE BOOK OF LEGENDS**
BY Dr. BAK NGUYEN & WILLIAM BAK

041- **THE BOOK OF LEGENDS 2**
BY Dr. BAK NGUYEN & WILLIAM BAK

086- **THE BOOK OF LEGENDS 3**
THE END OF THE INNOCENCE AGE
BY Dr. BAK NGUYEN & WILLIAM BAK

080- **1SELF**
REINVENT YOURSELF
FROM ANY CRISIS
BY Dr BAK NGUYEN

REBOOT -012
MIDLIFE CRISIS
BY Dr. BAK NGUYEN

THE LAZY FRANCHISE

HUMILITY FOR SUCCESS -051
BALANCING STRATEGY AND EMOTIONS
BY Dr. BAK NGUYEN

089- **THE CONFESSION OF
A LAZY OVERACHIEVER**
BY Dr BAK NGUYEN

THE ENERGY FORMULA -053
BY Dr. BAK NGUYEN

090- **TO OVERACHIEVE
EVERYTHING BEING LAZY**
CHEAT YOUR WAY TO SUCCESS
BY Dr BAK NGUYEN

AMONGST THE ALPHA -058
BY Dr. BAK NGUYEN & COACH JONAS DIOP

AMONGST THE ALPHA vol.2 -059
ON THE OTHER SIDE
BY Dr. BAK NGUYEN & COACH JONAS DIOP

THE 90 DAYS CHALLENGE -061
BY Dr. BAK NGUYEN

EMPOWERMENT -069
BY Dr BAK NGUYEN

003- **LEADERSHIP** -003
PANDORA'S BOX
BY Dr. BAK NGUYEN

THE MODERN WOMAN -070
TO HAVE IT HAVE WITH NO SACRIFICE
BY Dr. BAK NGUYEN & Dr. EMILY LETRAN

015- **FORCES OF NATURE**
FORGING THE CHARACTER
OF WINNERS
BY Dr BAK NGUYEN

ALPHA LADDERS -075
CAPTAIN OF YOUR DESTINY
BY Dr BAK NGUYEN & JONAS DIOP

040- **KRYPTO**
TO SAVE THE WORLD
BY Dr. BAK NGUYEN & ILYAS BAKOUCH

ALPHA LADDERS 2 -081
SHAPING LEADERS AND ACHIEVERS
BY Dr BAK NGUYEN & BRENDA GARCIA

MIRROR -085
BY Dr BAK NGUYEN

010 - **THE POWER OF YES**
VOLUME ONE: IMPACT
BY Dr BAK NGUYEN

LE RÊVE CANADIEN -013
D'IMMIGRANT À MILLIONNAIRE
par DR BAK NGUYEN

037 - **THE POWER OF YES 2**
VOLUME TWO: SHAPELESS
BY Dr BAK NGUYEN

CHOC -054
LE JARDIN D'EDITH
par DR BAK NGUYEN

046 - **THE POWER OF YES 3**
VOLUME THREE: LIMITLESS
BY Dr BAK NGUYEN

AFTERMATH -063
BUSINESS AFTER THE GREAT PAUSE
BY Dr BAK NGUYEN & Dr ERIC LACOSTE

087 - **THE POWER OF YES 4**
VOLUME FOUR: PURPOSE
BY Dr BAK NGUYEN

TOUCHSTONE -073
LEVERAGING TODAY'S
PSYCHOLOGICAL SMOG
BY Dr BAK NGUYEN & Dr KEN SEROTA

091 - **THE POWER OF YES 5**
VOLUME FIVE: ALPHA
BY Dr BAK NGUYEN

COVIDCONOMICS -074
THE GENERATION AHEAD
BY Dr BAK NGUYEN

092 - **THE POWER OF YES 6**
VOLUME SIX: PERSPECTIVE
BY Dr BAK NGUYEN

www.DrBakNguyen.com

AMAZON - BARNES & NOBLE - APPLE BOOKS - KINDLE
SPOTIFY - APPLE MUSIC

www.ingramcontent.com/pod-product-compliance
Lightning Source LLC
Chambersburg PA
CBHW060954230426
43665CB00015B/2204